F(

ADU

Stella is a miniature Jack Russell who leads a very colourful and adventurous life.

Never a dull moment is the order of the day as Stella leaps and bounds from one escapade to another.

It is written in a very tongue in cheek manner and the humour is very much off the wall and of a bizarre nature but upon reading I am sure you will have many comical moments as the events unfold.

ACKNOWLEDGMENTS

JANET DUFFY

ANDY CRAMPTON (RIP)

JASON ASHBY

LISA ASHBY

CHARLIE BRONSON SALVADOR

A TRUE INJUSTICE OF OUR OUR PENAL SYSTEM.

IN APPRECIATION OF ALL OF HIS CONTRIBUTIONS TO CHARITABLE CAUSES.

FREE THE ARTIST.

CHAPTER 1

I don't really know when I first realised I was different! I just know in my heart and mind that I had far more attitude than any other breed of dog. In actual fact it's probably where the term "a breed apart" actually originated from with me in mind.

My name is Stella and I am a miniature Jack Russell. The unrecognised breed of the canine world for many years and perhaps that's the reason for my bad temper.

Yes of course I have issues and would be the first to admit it but when you have listened to all of the criticism of my fellow terriers over the years the anger stems from there I guess.

Little dog syndrome seems to be the main accusation thrown in our direction each time we play up but in my opinion we are the ginger haired kid who gets bullied in school. We are the ginger nuts of the dog world.

In my opinion I am a very good natured dog with a very soft nature but I'm prepared to fight any other dog that says different L.O.L. Once you have read my story I am sure you will have a lot of sympathy towards me. I cannot remember much of my youth much the same as you humans are forgetful about the early years.

I can imagine I have been quite naughty and chewed everything in sight to piece s because to this day I still do that now and love to see the look on anyone's face when they return to their home after having left me unaccompanied for any great period of time.

I suppose all of the wanton destruction would have very much been a contributory factor in me being passed from home to home quite a few times. A regular orphan Annie I was for many years until I finally found an amicable owner who seems to understand my moods and mannerisms.

It would have perhaps been easy for him to come to terms with me and my erratic behaviour because he is a complete nutjob and very unpredictable himself. I shall explain in

I was already a little bit battered and bruised and took the decision to find a quiet corner and keep my noise to a minimum for the duration of my stay. A dog's life hey!!! Who would have it? It really was a tough up bringing but I learnt a lot out on the yard.

Of course I would be backed into my little corner but I learnt how to bare my teeth and stand my ground and of course a chain of command was set in place but they also knew I had very pincer type teeth and I would always manage to find the odd stray paw and cause a little damage. We gradually began to accept each other and I kept from going on the yard to a minimum and they preferred staying away from my place of refuge that nestled in the cosy corner of the yard.

My new owners weren't particularly neglectful but they needed to go out to work and they had obviously been pre-warned about the folly of leaving this "little bitch" unattended in the home. I had no course of appeal to be honest! I had dug my own grave with my earlier misdemeanours but in my defence I was a lovable little thing that was simply in need of constant attention.

I do finally find that love as you will discover in later chapters but for now I am giving you a brief summary of my formative years and what shaped me into the dog I am today. People can't have always considered me to be a demon dog or why would they have took the decision to breed with me.

Whilst covering this point could I tell you that hand on heart that the one and only time I have ever engaged in sexual activity the earth didn't exactly move for me. It was a very forgetful experience in a rather shabby garden shed, with a total stranger I might add and they say romance is dead hey. I never knew what his name was and it's a practice that certainly is not on any "to do" list of mine. I spend my days now humping any article of furniture or cushion that is available and find that much more preferable than the frothing at the mouth creature that was thrust upon me in that shed. But the outcome was three very adorable editions to my family and now here is another situation that concerns me, why is there a need to disband that family after a period of six weeks?

I go out for a toilet break with my family all snuggled in my basket and come back in to empty spaces. What is that all about? I pondered and pondered for days without coming greater detail later about my owner/father/carer who has proved to be very tolerant considering my eccentric behaviour.

From what I can recall I lived at three or four different family homes with lots of nice people and there would always be children within these homes and I would be very much loved. And why not? Because I have always been very cute simply by being as small as I am and in the eyes of many a child I would prove to be a very cuddlesome little creature.

Unfortunately though for different reasons I would soon be packed from one home to another. "Taxi for Stella" was always the order of the day which I always found to be very unsettling. A dog is for life never seemed to apply to me but hey ho I come to terms with it because at least the drastic decision to place me in a dogs' home was never taken at any time and maybe I've only myself to blame for some of the evictions. Maybe I should have realised my behaviour needed to be toned down a bit and a little less chewing of the furniture would help my cause but as much as I promised myself I would not cause no damage the net time I was left unattended within minutes of the door being closed I would once again be ragging cushions from side to side and spitting feathers everywhere.

Some dogs just sleep soundly while their owners are out but I am a mischievous Jack Russell and it's not in my nature to conform to any set agenda.

Different methods were put in place to curb my behaviour and I can recall periods of being confined to small cubbyholes within the household but I would quickly destroy anything I could lay my teeth into in there as well.

I classed it as being placed in a form of solitary confinement and Jesus Christ let's put things into perspective of course I was going to react badly and once there was nothing left to chew up I would make a start on the door and cause untold damage.

I was a playful little dog and confining me like that did little to improve my behaviour and I would be served yet again with notice to leave. I used to get called a "little bitch" quite often and I would flutter my little puppy eyes thinking it was a term of endearment.

There would be lots of hushed whispered conversations and it wouldn't be clear to me what was occurring until we went visiting other people and I would leap up wagging my tail when it was time to leave only for me to realise I would now be residing at this new address. Upon looking into the kitchen area and noticing my water and feed bowl in my own little spot the reality set in that I now lived here. Sometimes I used to think that I should have been born complete with a logbook!

There were other periods when I wasn't quite the fashionable pooch of the day and I'm sure lots of my other canine friends will have experienced the same outcome when the dreaded pug dogs came on the scene. Every home had to have one it seemed and I would watch from a distance while they now got all of the kisses that I used to get from the children.

Instantly I knew the time would be fast approaching when I would need to pack my suitcase and dressing gown yet again. I would be pretend to be accepting the situation but once everyone went to bed I would soon set about putting these young pretenders in their place.

Now don't get me wrong because I have always preferred to fight with all of the dogs much bigger than myself but I regarded these pugs as invading my territory and battle lines were definitely drawn when I observed one of them lapping away at MY water bowl. I inched over and caught him completely unaware and gave him the gentlest of nudges which served no purpose as he completely ignored my friendly warning and resumed his activities which resulted in a full on Tom and Jerry cartoon skirmish.

It must have become quite noisy because before I realised it everyone had got out of their beds and we was separated and placed in different rooms. The last thing I recalled before I began to settle down for the night was the dreaded "hushed whispers" again and I knew my days were numbered. I had become accustomed to it by now and even the children in Doctor Barnardo's had a more settled existence than me.

My next port of call was very much a testing ordeal with the realisation I was sharing a large patio come courtyard with two very big bull mastiff dogs and having been thrown up in the air a few times by this pair upon my arrival. I would always wait while they were both asleep, before I even considered going anywhere near the feeding bowls and even then I would crunch the dry feed as quietly as possible.

To be honest I didn't like the look of him but anything was preferable to that big yard with the two big bullies. I made myself at home instantly and began chewing on one of the cushions until I heard "Silly Bollox" shouting at me from the kitchen. Oops! I was only testing the water but it seems most humans all have the same rules. Jesus! What is it with you lot and your sacred head rests?

I'd already had a little mooch from room to room and on one of my excursions whilst jumping to the top of a chair I spotted what I now know to be the Coventry canal and instantly thought "I'm having some of that".

I hoped against hope I had gotten myself an owner who would trust me to not be on the leash and it was game on. I could sense I was going to enjoy my stay here.

For months I had been stuck on a back yard with limited exercise and yet here I was walking mile after mile down a canal towpath and with someone who seemed to enjoy my company and make a fuss of me.

I had certainly landed on my paws. He had no choice but to interact with me because on the few occasions he didn't I would play my ace card to attract his attention. SPLASH!!! In I went doing every swimming stroke you could imagine. Oh I can swim for hours like a little beaver and I can see his face screaming and red with rage but I go deaf when I'm in the water.

He is not to know that I am an Olympic swimmer and I can see the panic on his face with his continued failure to get me out. Don't worry yourself I will come out when I'm good and ready and you won't have to explain to people what you have done to their cute little dog whilst I am in your care.

Next time we are out for a walk perhaps you will keep me occupied by throwing a ball or something instead of testing girls who never get back to you anyway.

Today you have learnt rule number one NEVER take your eyes off Stella when there's water nearby. It is lucky for him that I CAN swim because he can't even swim a stroke useless git. Rule number one taken care of we now had to set about establishing the second one.

The sleeping arrangements. I'd had years of sheds, yards, cubby holes and even in the house it was always a downstairs arrangements and I had always had a craving to check out what sleeping on a bed was like. The first time I ventured up the stairs and sprang like

Had an interesting and varied life haven't I but it doesn't even really take shape until I introduce the love of my life. It took a few twists and turns but they were all worthwhile because it resulted in me meeting a funny man I call "Silly Bollox" in a fond way. My life is now complete! Don't get me wrong, I still get called a "little bitch" very often due to my behaviour but me and old "Silly Bollox" get on quite fine as you will discover!

CHAPTER 2

My new owners were going on holiday and needed minders for all three dogs and I was placed in the "safe keeping" to describe it loosely of my present keeper.

up with the answer. Had I been reported to social services for something I had been doing wrong? I hadn't misbehaved in the home for a long time so maybe my children had?

It is the same empty feeling for me as it is for a human to be having her baby taken from her to go into care. What is wrong with you people? Can you not see how I am pacing from room to room and searching everywhere? Years later I was considering contacting Jeremy Kyle show for him to help me to trace them but fortunately I met my present owner who knew all about my background and history and has helped me to re-establish some bond with them.

I also come across the "father" now and again but it is pointless asking him to step up to the plate regarding the children. I can see he still burns a candle for me he jumps up that excitedly when he sees me but as I stated previously my booty is now a no go area. As God is my judge I kid you not the fathers name is Bud and I suppose the likelihood is I will get teased until the end of my days about my shag BUD. Zip it back up Bud and don't even look in my direction!! You will not be getting any action with this little lady.

a leopard up and onto it I was over the moon how skilfully I had done it but all to no avail as I was scooped up and returned to the living room with the access door shut.

It was looking like game over until I brought the noise factor into play. I can't exactly howl like a wolf but I can whimper continually for however long it takes and would you believe it the exact same scoop that picked me up to take me downstairs had only got a return ticket on it and I found myself once again at the bottom of the cosy bed and I went straight to sleep thinking I really like being here with "Silly Bollox" as I rested my head on his ankles and felt pleasantly warm, loved and finally wanted.

I must have missed the recent bout of hushed whispers because it soon became clear that even though they were now back from holiday they had still not collected me in the hope that we have both become attached to each other.

I would watch him and he never seemed in no rush to ask if they were picking me up and I fervently hoped he had become attached because I certainly had. I wanted this one to be my final "Dad" and spend the rest of my days with him.

I had never been happier and when my previous owners finally showed up and a conversation took place in the kitchen it quickly became clear I was staying I could have done cartwheels but I remained reserved.

All the sympathetic pats on the head and comments such as "you'll be ok", I couldn't catch my breath of course I will be ok, vamoose adios please don't change your mind and in an instant they were gone. I wanted to shout to "Silly Bollox" get over that off license whilst it's still open and let's have a party.

Before I slept tonight I needed to have a set plan of action because for once in my life I had got what I wanted and I didn't want to fuck if up. The swimming in the canal would need to stop. Well!! Maybe still the odd dip but only if her seemed in a good mood.

So all was looking good and I'd need to find time to pop down to one of the charity shops and get myself a set of drawers of all of my clothes and toys.

My previous owners would call around occasionally and I suppose it eased their guilt a little but by now I was ruling the roost and strutting about like a peacock. All I needed was a nice silk dressing gown for Christmas and I would be the complete package.

By now I had my own basket in the living room and a chill out area under the stairs with a sleeping bag to lie on and as always I had my spot at the bottom of the bed each night.

I was no longer sharing a feed and scavenging for what little food I could get. I was more than happy to adopt this one as "my Dad" because he never let me down in any department and I quickly sensed he had quite a few issues of his own and hopefully I would be able to give him a little comfort at times when he needed it.

It wasn't to be all plain sailing and we would need to find our feet with each other.

Even if he had had a dog before it didn't show because he tended to not understand what came naturally to a little Jack Russell such as me. On one of our first walks he went absolutely ballistic when I got stuck down a hole. I could hear him screaming at the top of his voice whilst I thought "calm down dear! It's only a commercial". Obviously he thought HE was having a little bit of high drama, what did he think I felt like with myself firmly wedged in this tiny hole with my cute little arse hanging out for all to see.

I'm meant to come out of the hole with a rabbit on display in a similar vain to a magician with a top hat. Unfortunately, things do not always go according to plan and anyway it's as much your fault as mine because he should have a ferret down his trousers and then I don't get to do the work of two.

I finally get out of the hole rather less white than I went down it and all the way home I had to listen to his constant mutterings of complaint so when I saw just about the most perfect pile of fox shit I had ever seen I thought it would be wise not to flip on my back and have a good roll in it although I looked back on several occasions in envy knowing another dog on the estate would claim that for the backward flip and roll.

It shouldn't have mattered to be honest because on his incessant rant I had clearly heard bath mentioned so it was patently obvious I was about to be going to be going under the tap AGAIN so why an extra addition on my back to be shampooed should create a problem is beyond me!

Oh yes indeedy I also had the best shampoos and toiletries so don't be one bit shocked. The only problem there was in that department is yours truly, the author, was not too keen on bath time even though I did smell slightly rank after a few circuits in the canal water.

I had certainly landed on my feet here and I should rein myself in a bit before I cut my throat and lost it all. I tried putting in a bit of extra effort to please him and one day when I dropped a hedgehog at his feet he swiftly kicked it into the water not in the least bit pleased. I didn't actually hunt and catch it and although "my Dad" wasn't in the least bit pleased it gave me an insight into the do's and don'ts. I made a mental note that "Dad don't like dead hedgehogs" and not to bring him one again. It was obviously a rabbit he wanted or nothing. He didn't seem to understand that a rabbit can run fast and is very difficult for me to catch and being as how it was looking like I was banned from going down holes how the fuck did he expect this to be resolved? It's much easier to catch a hedgehog and simplified even more by the fact it was dead.

No! I wasn't cut out to be a hunting dog. There's no doubt with adequate training it might have happened but sod that now I'm tasting the good life I'm putting my feet up; it's all about the food, walks and rest.

I'm more of a town girl and can often be found outside one of the department stores in the town and I've become quite famous and everyone knows my name.

What a leap I had taken hey, from being a scared little dog cowering in the corner of a yard to overnight celebrity status? Everyone knows me and greets me warmly and I had that many friends I felt it only right to own my own Facebook account which is proving quite popular and gaining friends at a frantic pace. It's one of the main incentives I have for the decision to write my memoirs.

Be prepared for many incidents and anecdotes that will probably make your toes curl but it's a story that needs telling.

I am not just a regular run of the mill dog. Rin Tin Tin, Lassie and Snowy are all established names in the canine world, I agree, but I will tell you stories throughout that you'd never believe. Hold my paw and let the journey begin.

Jack Russell's may not have been accepted for many years but I can assure you that after all of my revelations you will see us in a different light altogether.

Oh I'm a very naughty little bitch at times but aren't we all girls? Although I felt I was naughty I hadn't taken time to take two steps back and appreciate how much more naughty "Silly Bollox" was and how eventful my story was likely to be. It didn't take long for me to get the first inkling of what lay ahead.

CHAPTER 3

Bang! Crash! The front door came in with a thunderous noise and perhaps ten strangers were in the flat looking very much like the Salvation Army band but by the stern look on their faces they definitely hadn't come to sing.

Not that I wanted them to! They had already made way too much noise for my liking. My little chill out room meant I would be the first to come into contact with them due to its close proximity to the front door.

This was my very first encounter with the police and I was fearful it wouldn't be a pleasant experience. I had seen Dad come past sheepishly with handcuffs on his wrists and I was now concerned for my own safety and was tempted to head for the door. I am a very quick mover over the first ten metres and they would have soon realised it was impossible to catch me in full flight. I decided not to be hasty for the time being because I seemed to be getting lots of "cute dog" pats and strokes from the officers in attendance. By now "my Dad" had been placed in the back of the police car and I witnessed the few officers who had been left behind conducting a thorough search from room to room.

I went and sat in front of my treat cupboard packed out with the finest delicacies the town had to offer but which I was only allowed on special occasions. Foolishly the officer had noticed how I sat by the cupboard and possibly convinced himself I was tipping him off in some shape or form. He dropped to his knees and shone his torch inside and after taking bag after bag out once he had checked the contents he would place the items on the kitchen floor whilst he stuck his head deeper into the confined space. Oh boy! The temptation was too much to pass by as I swept my favourite bag up with my teeth hurried to conceal them inside my chill out room. Upon my return he kept saying "what is it boy where is it boy?" Uuum! For one thing you need to take a closer look because the last thing I am is boy!

Excuse me officer I thought to myself you are certainly not CID material I overheard the remaining officers saying "what are we going to do about the dog?" Instant panic set in and I thought this is where social services become involved and I get placed in care.

I thought I was going to be remanded to Battersea dogs home and I had committed no crime.

I was glad I had not taken the decision to bolt because the decision was taken between them to put me some water out and then just leave me to roam about until my Dad got bailed later.

Reading between the lines he hadn't done anything drastic enough for him to be in custody for any great length of time so after yet more "cute dog" pats I was left to fend for myself for the remainder of the day.

Bonus!! The treat cupboard had been left ajar so I nuzzled that open further with my nose and feasted my eyes on a veritable Aladdin's cave which I would return to sooner rather than later.

I went from room to room to assess the damage and what could have possibly brought about this rude intrusion.

I came across what I thought was Dad's "Glastonbury" tent but upon closer inspection there were remnants of some plants he had been growing. Wait a minute I recognise that aroma. It had been circulating the flat for months. All the time I had been thinking the stench was coming from me and all of my unauthorised swims in the canal.

You sly old fox!! So this is where you were coming for an hour at a time when you threw my play ball to occupy me in the living room.

On a realistic note I had to appreciate that this shady activity was possibly the source of income that had been paying for my full groom and nail jobs and certainly the treats.

Oh my God! The treats I quickly sprinted down the stair well taking the stairs two and three at a time. If the loss of income was going to affect the distribution of my tasty morsels I would need to secrete the remainder away whilst I had the opportunity which I did there and then.

Day quickly turned into night and I found myself alone in the dark and in desperate need of a toilet break and just when I was considering finding a spot for a tiny slut drop the door opened and in walked my Dad muttering profanity after profanity.

I would safely say this was the worst mood I had ever seen him in at any time before or since so after I had been given a little walk I took the decision to stay low key and keep my head down.

I went to my little retreat under the stairs and set about tidying my room with a little dustpan and brush to gather all the little bits of bone shrapnel that had been building up for a while.

It was obviously going to affect our finances as I listened to him speak to different people down the phone and I was fearful where this would leave my position within the household.

I didn't think it would lead to me being actually homeless and so it proved but it soon became clear we had now fallen on hard times.

It was fortunate I had hidden the goodies that I had earlier to boost my intake because overnight I found myself on the bleeding Atkins Diet or something. I would make my way to my dining area only to be greeted by a few fish fingers for Christ sake!

If things didn't pick up I could visualise tomatoes and lettuce leafs in the mix and I may as well begin to attend weight watchers meetings.

Now don't get me wrong I would be the first to admit I needed to lose a few pounds with all the rich living of the previous months but I was struggling to go from one extreme to the other.

Times were hard and when we would go the local Co-op I would watch from a distance as Dad slipped a jar of coffee into his pocket with no intention of paying. I had never committed a crime in my life but I thought in for a penny in for a pound as I ran from the store with an average sized block of cheese in my mouth. I could hear lots of laughs behind me as I raced and raced to put some distance between me and the store.

When Dad finally caught up with me I fully expected him to be angry with me but instead rather foolishly he kept patting my head and asking "where's the cheese" and "good girl" in a very complimentary fashion until he realised I no longer had the proceeds. Deary me! He now thinks I have lost it during the chase. Are you for real? I was fucking starving and the cheese has long since been devoured.

It's not like I'm going to be wanting a bleeding cup of your coffee is it? It's not like it was the crime of the century and nor did they need to post wanted stickers throughout the area as everyone throughout the estate knew it was us and the message was relayed that we were now barred from the store.

My first crime hadn't been a memorable one but at least I'd not spent a night in the cells. On the plus side I was no longer hungry.

In future I would leave all of the solutions to our poverty trap to the mastermind himself; the one and only "Silly Bollox". After all he had enough coffee to last him a week while he hatched out another of his super plans.

I had only been with him a matter of weeks and already had my first brush with the law and been involved in my own little theft. Not exactly a crime wave but I could sense already it was going to be rather interesting living alongside "Silly Bollox".

With me being very small I would chuckle inwardly imaging headlines of a "mini" crime wave in the local newspapers I definitely would be quite easy to pick out on any identity parade.

The big problem with finance appeared to be because Dad had to pay for an unused bedroom and he was regarded as under occupying the premises and had the choice of downsizing or the inevitable unfair tax on that room which amounted to £20 a per week. It wasn't possible to register me as an additional tenant because I am only a dog.

I had never got political my whole dog life and all I had done was run around being silly and chasing a ball but what i did understand was this cruel policy affected everyone in turn. I didn't want to get involved in the finance side of it. Cash flow is for humans to deal with. But when the end result is fish fingers still putting in a regular appearance on my menu then I will become an activist against any tory policies that affect me and will resist till my dying bark. If I see one more bleeding piece of fish I will scream and wake the whole block. I'm a bloody dog for Christ sake not a bleeding cat!

Things began to pick up after a short while and I would always eavesdrop on Dad's phone conversations and it was very much sounding like a holiday was on the cards. Yippee!! Another first!! I had never been anywhere other than Nuneaton and it seemed a whole new adventurous world was opening up. I began to watch all of the holiday programmes on the TV and would sit in front of it, glued to the screen and try and guess our location.

I had certainly let my imagination run wild with me once the realisation kicked in that we would simply be visiting Dad's place of birth which was Dewsbury in Yorkshire. In the short space of time I had been around him I had quickly gathered that he spoke differently to other people I had lived with in this area.

What I wasn't aware of though was his birth place was a sort of place that time had forgotten and probably where dinosaurs had definitely roamed free. Apparently the place I was going to visit had a never ending supply of Jack Russell's who would definitely do a day's work as most of the public houses would confirm with row upon row of freshly skinned rabbits adorning the tables. Sod that I thought! I'm a lady and I am coming on holiday and have no intention of breaking any of my nails.

I had already met some savoury characters in my life but Yorkshire was about to take that to a completely different level. I was hoping the North was ready for me in all of my glory but it would be a complete role reversal as I would need to stand open mouthed at some of the sights and people I was about to see. A proper eye opener indeed! Hey up lad! Eeeh bah gum, let the journey begin. Maybe I would find a little romance while I'm up there! Lock up your whippets Stella is coming to Yorkshire.

CHAPTER 4

I'd never seen a train before and about jumped into my Dad's arms as the first intercity non-stop express hurtled through in the blink of an eye. I was on a high with the realisation I was not required to pay for my ticket to travel. The journey had barely begun and already I felt I had celebrity status. At this rate surely I would be expected to walk the red carpet upon my arrival.

I stared excitedly out of the window all throughout the journey until I finally fell asleep for a short while. When I roused a little and once again looked out, all of the buildings now seemed to have an eerie grey about them and much different to the town we left. All of the "Churches" had strange turrets at the top of them the like I had never seen before. How long had I been asleep? Where were we in Baghdad? Everyone seemed to have long beards and long flowing robes. I'd watched Sinbad on the television a few times and this very much reminded me of that setting. For fucks sake Dad! Where have you brought me and more importantly can we leave when we decide to? Even Dad seemed shocked at the change in the area and if he is took a back then I am also quite happy to hide behind his legs and just have an occasional peep between his ankles.

We had entered a Muslim stronghold akin to Helman Province and I had no intention of barking even once for fear of drawing attention to myself. Congratulations Dad! You are an expert in choosing holiday destinations. Everyone else heads for Butlin's but not you!

Get me to my room now "Silly Bollox" and I won't be coming out until the end of the week. Jesus! I wish I had bought my own suicide vest from Poundland now to bring up with me.

The taxi driver spoke in a tongue very unrecognisable to me and suddenly home and my little bolthole with the hidden treats seemed a million miles age. Oh dear God! Please for the comforts of home and I promise never to steal cheese again. I was nervous and on edge but I visibly relaxed when I see the driver in conversation with my Dad and both of them laughing quite regular throughout the journey. He seemed to be enjoying my Dad's company but I still kept peeping over his shoulder to confirm he didn't have a vest and detonator on him.

Where the fuck am I and how come I'm stuck in yet another situation with "Silly Bollox". I'd even begun to look back fondly on my time with the two bull mastiffs in the yard and would have given anything at the moment to be back there getting beat up on a daily basis.

We were met by Dad's friend at the end of the journey and a man called Mick Fox was going to be my co-owner for the week and suddenly all of my fears disappeared as Mick treat me as royalty.

Other friends called and one called Caron Morton who worked at a veterinary surgeons also called around and it was plain to see she was a dog lover through and through. She motioned for me to come and sit by her and told me she had a treat for me in her bag. My tail wagged in anticipation, are you watching this "Silly Bollox" I bet she's not going to pull out a fucking stack of fish fingers from her bag. I would stay close to Caron and Mick for the rest of my stay because Caron would be able to help me with any travel sickness I got being as how she worked at the vets.

Mick is built like the side of a house and if anything got detonated while I was sat with him nothing could possibly hit me so I would sit between them and feel safe while I watched Emmerdale.

I'd read in papers that Yorkshire people eat anything wrapped in newspapers and one of their delicacies was a thing called tripe from the inside of a cow. I had never seen any of it while I was up there but I can confirm that they eat everything in sight. In actual fact the only reason Jack Russell's don't get eaten is because they are the grafters who fill the stew pot. If they didn't have such a high success rate I could well imagine they would find themselves between two slices of bread but at least I had a safe passage while I was up there in that respect because the little hunting dogs are held in the highest esteem. I hope nobody seriously thought I'd be putting in a shift of grafting because I'm up here on holiday and to put my paws up. Hadn't I enough on my plate needing to keep a close eye on the Muslim extremists Dewsbury was renowned for.

Let me assure you that the nearest I would be going to a rabbit would be my share I would be eating from the pot. If I was a lucky girl I'd maybe get a slab of tripe to dip in my gravy.

Yorkshire I could see was likely to be a very testing time but I would need to take it on the chin and just pray that we both got home in one piece. All of the shopkeepers had very large machetes and I had no reason to doubt that should anyone attempt to steal even one item there was a strong possibility of losing at least a few fingers. The machetes could clearly be seen hanging on a nail at the back of the counter to act as a deterrent and there was certainly no need to employ store detectives L.O.L.

On the few occasions I had ventured out I was in need of my toilet duties and also began to mark my territory and very quickly had a few skirmishes with the local mongrels. Not a problem! They were soon put in their place.

There were crossbreeds the likes I'd never seen before and I was beginning to think I was in an episode of Doctor Who or some science fiction thriller. I preferred staying in and reading a book or watching a bit of TV. No way on this earth were any of these hybrids mounting me? I dread to think what the end product would look like. For some strange reason there didn't seem to be as many strays as there was back home though and there was rumours a plenty that many got served up at the local takeaways. Not necessarily politically correct I know should it be true but for sure I wasn't prepared to take that chance and would rush to do what I needed to do and get back indoors at the earliest opportunity and get myself back on Mick's settee.

I would stare out of the window on regular occasions and let my imagination run wild as to why there seemed to be no cats to chase or dogs to fight or even pigeons to scatter. I held frightening thoughts of gangs of multi-cultural immigrants' roaming the neighbourhood with meat cleavers and lots of hessian sacks and I promised myself that a lady of standing such as myself would not be meeting such a fate.

Lots of Dad's friends called to see him whilst he was at Mick's and also a young man who looked very similar to him who I quickly gathered was his son who bore the same name David. So obviously Dad hadn't been shy in his earlier years and must have had a girl in every port because he seemed to have children spread throughout the country.

I would never venture out unaccompanied but on the occasions I did go out with Dad or his friends there I would enjoy the wide open areas that Yorkshire has to offer and would run freely on these days and would certainly now feel I was on a holiday of sorts.

It wasn't bikini weather for me but would readily admit on these outings I was certainly having a lot of fun and began to enjoy myself and relax a little. On one journey while we were making our way back home we passed close to the local refuse tip. I ran towards what I believed to be a large black cat and thought that maybe its deemed to be lucky but your luck is about to run out but fortunately for me it managed to escape.

I had listened to Dad's friends as they complimented him on my natural hunting instincts and it was at this point I realised that in actual fact I had been chasing one of the largest rodents i am ever likely to encounter. Sweet Jesus! Are you people mental? Had I known it was a rat I would have changed gear and put my cute little arse into reverse gear and ran for the Yorkshire hills and wouldn't have stopped until I'd crossed the Pennines. That bleeding thing was twice the size of me and I would have been off like lightning.

The conversation between them seemed to revolve around "working dogs" and I thought that definitely needs nipping in the bud. Work didn't even figure in any of my calculations. Put your ferrets back down your trousers. For fucks sake! I'm up here on vacation aren't I so forget all this talk of hunting and working. This rat would have been the heavy weight champion of the refuse tip for however many previous years and if anyone in their right mind thought I was about to climb in the ring with him then you needed to think again! Not a job that was top of my list I'm afraid and if there was a problem with rodents in the area then feel free to borrow my phone and drop the pied piper a text. I had a lucky escape because Roland would have torn me limb from limb.

Anyway all this talk of work had made me hungry and I felt it was time to be heading home and getting the cutlery out. Also the quicker we got away from this area the better because it would be safe to say that Roland had many similar sized relatives in the vicinity and I wanted to finish "work" early for the day. I was clocking out and finishing my "shift" and would prefer it if we did not walk this route again. Yes it was very scenic but in future I'd prefer if you brought your air rifles with you and whatever "work" needed doing then do it from a distance and keep me out of harm's way.

In actual fact by now I felt in need of one of my full grooms and pamper sessions but I doubted very much that there would be any great amount of pooch parlours in this God forsaken part of the country which was created for men of a very robust nature.

I took the decision to just wing it until we got back to our own home town and just rough it with the local natives. If nothing else it had been an adventure of sorts and I would have some lasting memories to take back with me and I had met some very nice people. To this day I do not know what the purpose of the visit was but knowing my Dad as I do it would have been something shady and of a criminal nature.

The holiday came to an end and we all parted at the train station with a lot of fond farewells. I mounted the train with a spring in my step in the knowledge I had made many new friends and convinced myself I had been more than a match for terrorists, dog nappers and mutant rats. In my mind I had been a very brave little warrior but in my heart I knew different. I promised myself I would toughen up by the time I visited again.

Perhaps it was time to start using my local gym to beef myself up a bit. Yet again it was free train travel for me and I felt I had reached a celebrity status. The train was quite crowded and the rule was I would need to give up my seat which was no big deal as my Dad placed me up in the overhead luggage rack.

The last thing I remember as I fell asleep with my head hanging over the edge was the cute comments about me from the other passengers. I soon nodded off in my cosy little recess. We were finally homeward bound! Farewell Yorkshire, I was sure I would return another time.

CHAPTER 5

The train journey passed without any incident and we arrived back in the Midlands early afternoon and some of Dad's friends met us at the front of the station.

I could have staked all of my money I had hid under the stairs for a rainy day that our first port of call would have been one of the nearby public houses and I would have certainly doubled my money.

A lot of back slapping hand shaking and high fives seemed to be occurring and everyone was in high spirits as round after round of drinks were being shouted up from the not so pretty barmaid who had a face hat told you she would much rather be somewhere, anywhere else as she continued to paint her nails and enter cyber space via her smart phone. It reminded me that I would need a smart phone of my own in the not to near future.

My Dad was an old dinosaur who got by year in year out with his old Nokia phone and I had "borrowed" it a few times when he was asleep and I was bored and couldn't sleep because I had slept most of the day. Not a lot to occupy me there to be honest except a standard boring game of snakes. I would wait my moment and get myself a smart phone as soon as the opportunity came about which as it happens wouldn't be long.

I began to be a little embarrassed with Dad and this company as their behaviour became more and more raucous. It was only a matter of time before they got asked to leave the pub. "Standard practice"! It ALWAYS happened. Nobody would ever want this little circles company for very long. In actual fact neither did I want them back at the flat but it was inevitable that was going to be the end setting.

All of them drunk and telling the same stories, listening to the same songs as what they did on every other occasion. Yawn! Yawn! It bored me at other times but today I had just come on a very long journey and would have preferred a peaceful night.

As soon as we entered the flat I made for my little room not even bothering to unpack. In my opinion they had, all of them, consumed more than enough alcohol but had chosen to stop off at the off license to replenish their stocks. Within in minutes it was exactly how I anticipated as "I want to be adored" by the Stone Roses reverberated around the flat and echoed off the walls in my room. It would be pointless trying to get any sleep so I mooched into the living room. What a bunch of nutjobs I thought looking at them with their arms around each other singing "I wanna be adored" in unison.

There seemed to be no shortage of money so hopefully a little fine steak should be putting in an appearance over the next few days.

The music finally abated and nobody's energy levels could even muster a sing song together.

By the time it ended a couple of town foxes were roaming up and down the main road outside making for the bin area. I had watched them do it before as I perched on top of the armchair by the bay window. They had seen me before and felt no threat from me, nor I from them. We all needed to eat and if i could share my forth coming steaks I would.

But getting back to the reprobates in here I went from one to the other and although the odd eye here and there remained open these idiots were completely out of the game. I put my two paws onto the coffee table and smelt the contents of the ashtray. Oh dear!! That aroma was very much like the one that used to come from the "Glastonbury" tent upstairs. Now I understood why the music had ceased far earlier than what it normally would.

Baron, a lad, who is usually the last man standing is the first one to check out because if he is gone then the rest of them are certainly finished and right enough he was sprawled, cross eyed in one of the chairs.

Gaz Kent was the next one I gave the once over and I even sat on his chest while I went eye to eye and nose to nose with him. Not a flicker. As I climbed down from Gaz I noticed his smart phone was hanging loose from his hand and so I gently removed it and took it to conceal in my room with my other possessions I had previously purloined.

I should have been born a magpie because I would lay claim to anything shiny. I would never take notes from the coffee table and then I never seemed to draw much attention. The phone was the biggest item I had ever stolen and would certainly be missed but fortunately the assumption in the morning by Gaz was he must have left it in the pub or taxi. The world is now my oyster and I would take full advantage of it. My favourite programmes that I often missed I could now watch on catch up, happy days.

I hadn't been mistaken about our financial status because over the next few weeks everything took a turn for the better. The fish fingers had been laid to rest R.I.P to the fish fingers. A big lamb shank got threw into my room and I did a cartwheel, two hand springs and a forward roll and landed in the exact same spot as the shank.

The high life suited me down to the ground but I began to have a few problems with my plumbing. We girls know what mean; it shouldn't have been period pains because I was quite old now and I thought they were well and truly finished with. OMG! Maybe I needed a hysterectomy!

Dad got in touch with "Auntie Caron" the lady we had met up the north and a few discussions took place about maybe I had picked up a bug in Yorkshire. State of the fucking refuse tip and the rats roaming about I'd be very surprised if I hadn't!! Caron, kindly, sent some worming tablets through the post just in case my problem was in that department. She gave him instructions what to do as does everyone who meets him to be honest. He is not exactly the sharpest chisel in the tool box. I would watch him each morning crushing the tablet to mix in my food to make sure I consumed it.

Jesus Christ! Dearest Father! I am a big girl now and have watched you and your friends roll notes up that often or sniff through a straw that I'm quite sure should you crush my worming tablet up to a fine powder that I could do the same.

The decision was reached that I was under the weather and needed lots of bed rest. Were they having a fucking laugh, bed rest at this address?

As quick as one taxi pulled away another one pulled up; each of them carrying nuttier passengers than the previous ones. Come in lads, make yourselves at home and let me guess you all "wanna be adored". Pump up the volume "Silly Bollox" your guests have arrived.

I wasn't too bothered that I'd got to go to my room yet again because I was still learning how to use my phone and instead of listening to all of the experts I could google my symptoms. I would be able to teach myself all sorts now, which would be a great help considering I'd had no schooling of any sort.

I'd even bought a Teenage Ninja Turtle satchel when I was little planning around having a little Tupperware box with all of my treats in for when I attended school but it never ever came to it.

I just accepted that maybe I was outside this or that catchment area knowing how petty the education system could be nowadays but it didn't much matter now because I had access to all the education I needed.

With a little Instagram, snapchat and plenty of fish thrown in of course L.O.L. I had a few days in my room and some very long feverish sleeps and as I awoke one day and could hear voices from the living room, I ambled in fully expecting it to be my Dad's usual cronies and I got the shock of my life.

I kid you not! Gospel truth! Sat there in attendance was KEN LOACH the world renowned film producer. I was speechless and very awestruck. It turned out that Ken was making a film called I Daniel Blake and it concerned all of the government sanctions by the tory government and my Dad was to get a mention in it because of him suffering hardship through being a bedroom tax victim.

My Dad! A film star! Wow!! Well not exactly as it turns out but his name is in the credits at the end of the film. My Dad often speaks highly of Ken and his friend Paul Laverty and he is proud to have been of any assistance to this duo.

My Dad wrote two bestselling books himself that can be found on Amazon and I just hope he doesn't become jealous if mines also a best seller. I've already got the vision in my head of me book signing down at Waterstones.

Everyone in town knows me anyway because I am always down there and everyone knows my name so I suppose you could say I am already famous. None of you knew I could write though did you? You learn something new every day hey.

I will probably have lots of difficulty completing a book with all of the noisy distractions in and around the flat so I will probably look online to find me a country retreat. Preferably with hot tubs and an idyllic lake with swans, I enjoy going head to head with any swans. I annoy and annoy them until they spread their wings in anger. I do it with the ones on the canal out the back here. It must look quite comical me about twelve inches high whey they try and engulf me in their wings.

I intend completing this project now I have started it but my little paw is dropping off already and I've barely started. But as they say "no pain no gain".

CHAPTER 6

I'm hoping my book is a success as I haven't given much thought to an alternative career as of yet although I feel I could make a really good sniffer dog for the police. I would obviously need to work away from the area because I wouldn't want to arrest any of Dad's friends and also it wouldn't be very difficult for me to find any local stashes as I've already been to most of their homes on social visits and know all of their hiding places.

Oh I'm good at sniffing things out because my nose is 100 times more powerful than humans. When Dad used to have mad parties and certain individuals would claim they had no drugs left Dad would simply give me the "search" command and it would not take me long before I sat down in front of them wagging my tail and unnerving them. I would get a pat on the head and be promised a treat shortly. I would be happy with that but please for fucks sake don't throw a bleeding fish finger in my direction as a reward.

I believe I could easily get into the police force because I haven't got a criminal record. I've never even spent one night in a police cells. I suppose you could say I've sailed close to the edge but I've never been cuffed up.

My eyes maybe failing with age but my nose is as finely tuned as a violin. It's in better shape than my Dad's though all day long which would be quite easy considering all of the toxins he has put up his for all of the years. The silly twat!

I'm not sure Dad would be pleased with that choice of career though so maybe not.

Imagine a scenario in years to come if I had to sit by him in an arrest situation. That would go down like a lead balloon as I waved him off to the cells. Call it pay back for all of the fish fingers you sad act. L.O.L. No! That's a bad thought and I'd rather not go there.

He has always been good to me and I could never imagine a day being apart from him although now there was a little money about it didn't take him long to jump on a flight to Tenerife with just about everything packed in his case …. Except me!

I've never felt so sad sat at the door believing right up to the very last minute he wouldn't ever even consider going anywhere without me. But he had booked without me. I googled everything to do with Tenerife and it seemed right up my street. You Bastard! I thought and I was tempted to text him but he would have known I'd nicked his friends phone then and I preferred living in my secret world.

For the next 48 hours I sat and sulked in my room because I didn't even like the dog sitters he had got in for me. I would wake with the driest throat imaginable but it would be pointless going to the water bowl because none had been put out, yet again! I thought I had another five days of this and was feeling very sorry for myself when, unexpectedly I heard Dad's voice in the living room.

I have never experienced the joy of that day and after he had a shout out at the two people who had neglected me and he threw them out I spent the rest of the evening jumping so high I was landing on his shoulders.

I had thought he had missed me so much that he had took the decision to catch an early flight home to me but once I listened in on his phone conversations it soon became clear that a fight had broken out at the hotel he was staying at and the police had been sent for and Dad had to get out of the hotel very quickly and he had spent the night sleeping on the beach until he could get an early morning flight out of there and away from the situation.

It was his birthday that morning as well so you had to feel a little sorry for him but having said that he is the one that always finds himself in these situations. 48 hours in Tenerife and he has to run for the airport before he gets a Spanish police boot up his arse! You couldn't make this shit up!

By the end of this book I'm sure you will, by then, realise why he has the tag name "Silly

Bollox". Never has a term seemed so applicable to a man as this one. But he is my Dad, my soul mate and my "Silly Bollox" and we are a team and inseparable.

He has written his books and now it's my turn to tell you a no punches held story. Of course it's been a white knuckle ride for a lot of the time but I wouldn't have swapped one minute of my time with him. Even though he never even brought me a fridge magnet back from Spain or some little present.

At least there was still quite a bit of money knocking about due to the holiday finishing earlier than expected. The fridge freezer and tin cupboard were both packed to the rafters and we could afford to have both the fire and the central heating on at the same time. Talk about greenhouse effect! It was like being in the Tropics in here. So much so I was just strutting about in my bra and pants I'd got from an Ann Summers party.

Things were about to get a whole lot warmer though as a letter was posted in from the council stating that they was about to put an eviction order in place because of the cannabis grow in the premises. Oh dear, drama yet again!

Fortunately my Dad was getting treated under the Mental Health Act and was regarded as vulnerable and so not a lot could be done regarding the matter. Phew! A stay of execution and he was given a years' probation by the council to correct his behaviour.

It wasn't typed out in print as such but I presumed I was now responsible for his actions and it wasn't a task I was particularly relishing due to his unpredictable behaviour but it would need doing if we were to stay in the property.

I would make a point of barking or snarling if I noticed he hadn't taken his medication. On one occasion when I thought he had but in actual fact hadn't in the blink of an eye he had charged out of the door semi-nude with a machete and chased two bailiffs along the landing, down the stairwell and by the time I had caught up with him he was on the bonnet of the bailiffs van and attempting to smash the windscreen. I kid you not!

These were the type of events I would need to watch for on a daily basis. I knew he had a mental history and had been in a few hospitals but some of these incidents were extreme to say the least.

He was and still is good to me but I needed to watch for his silent mutterings to himself to give me any indication of the impending outburst. The lunatics have taken over the asylum or if not they have certainly taken over this flat but I loved him and he was he owner I wanted to spend the rest of my life with. Someone had to put up with it and it was looking like I had drawn the short straw.

He had met a few female "friends" along the way but whichever one it was he would soon put a spoke in that and if he didn't and it was a female I didn't like then I would cause the rift. On the odd occasion when one or two would actually make it to the bedroom, they would need to get accustomed to the little lump at the bottom of the bed by their feet. Once they propped up on their elbows wondering what it was, there was always two ways of dealing with matters. I could wag my tail and give a half cute smile or I could bare my teeth with a silent snarl. Your call lady!

I would usually be accepted into the fold and we were all one big happy family, as a little girl I had always dreamed of catching the thrown flowers at a wedding but the nearest I had come to that so far was when Dad would suddenly vanish under the quilt and before you knew it a pair of lacy little panties would be winging their way around the bedroom for me to catch.

If I liked the female individual then obviously no further action would be needed but if I disliked her then you bet your bottom dollar they would be shredded by yours truly and to be found all tattered and torn in different sections of the home.

Perhaps there was a little jealousy involved I suppose because on many an occasion if there was visitors to the home I felt I was being ignored I would resort to my usual practice of going where Dad was sat and lock onto his arm and hump it feverishly.

Oh I've seen a few guests spit their tea out with that one or drop their biscuits which was another bonus because I would eat that shortly. If I thought any guest had outstayed their welcome then for sure "the hump" has them headed for the door and if it doesn't appear to work I would step up the action and hump their arm or leg. A sure fire winner!! Bye then! Catch you next time you visit although I doubt you will be in any hurry to call again. But joking aside romance just never seemed to be at the top of any agenda with my Dad.

It was obvious he had met some very bad, evil sorts and he would be forever licking his wounds. He just never made any effort with them no more and just seemed content in his own little world. It mattered little or nothing to me if he paired off with any one of them because I know within a few weeks they would realise he had a few mental health issues. It didn't make him a bad person and I for one was happy I'd found him. I want for nothing!

If it was a choice of a weekly shop from Iceland or a groom for me I would always be put first so should he need the comfort of me at any time due to him being a little stressed then I would instantly spring, like an antelope, into his lap. We were a team a very formidable team.

I didn't know about crime until I'd come across him and I'm not sure I want to know too much anyway but it seemed a little late for that. We were the Bonnie and Clyde of the human world. I could deal with all of it as long as I didn't end up on a prison exercise yard.

The one thing that you could be stone cold certain of is the police would definitely receive a "no comment" from me. We had formed a good bond and I'd finally found my little niche in life for sure. The only way was up!!

CHAPTER 7

The situation suited me down to the ground because I was of the exact same opinion as Dad and in no need of a partner. My circumstances were a little different I suppose because I had only had that one sexual encounter but it had put me off for life.

Down the years I have lost count of the dogs I have had to terrorise for even daring to come close up and sniffing my rear end. No! That games not for me at all on the one occasion I had the pups I told you about if I'd have known in advance exactly how sordid the breeding process was I'd have probably grown a few cannabis plants myself to pay for a little IVF treatment.

I'm a pretty girl and very lady like when I wish to be and have had a string of admirers but the dating game isn't for me I'm afraid. All of that breeding game with everyone stood around ogling to confirm that the deed has been done. It was like being in a strip club down Soho there were that many voyeurs hanging around watching me lose my virginity.

To top it off the father not present at the birth. Sound familiar girls? I had long since put it behind me now and dread my daughter going through the same. I have just found out recently I am a proud Grandma now. Not bad for a twelve year old hey and I plan to be around for many more years yet. Most days I walk a minimum of ten miles a day with my Dad and I am far and away the fittest dog on the estate. I am never ever indoors and have a very hectic social life and can be seen in all of the pubs and clubs regular.

Problem is my Dad never knows when it's time to go home, it's not rare for us to be seen walking home in the early hours of the morning. Him walking in figures of eights and me just walking direct as an arrow and in desperate need of my basket. I didn't mind being in the pub when I was younger but would rather it wasn't in my diary now.

Many of my funny moments have come in pubs though if I'm honest. I can remember an occasion when England were playing Scotland at football and some of the local Scottish lads turned up in "skirts" or kilts as they prefer to call them and I had long been aware of the rumour of what or what not is worn underneath their dresses!!! I am certainly small enough to get right below the few Scottish lads that were in there and as much as I'd like to tell you I seen a few Loch Ness monsters staring down at me it was far from the case as I peered at what looked like slugs coming out of hibernation. Inside one of them I am sure I witnessed a pair of very lacy black panties as I recoiled in horror and there was no way I was delving back under there for any further investigation.

I was taken aback and for the remainder of the game concealed myself under the pool table and only ventured out to steal the snacks that had been laid out. I came to conclusion that yes indeed the Scotch are a strange breed and brought some strange habits with them once they had scaled Hadrian's Wall.

Now I didn't exactly have a "to do" list but things just happened by chance and because Dad had been out all day, with me in tow, and then the local night club was suggested as a final port of call I found myself placed inside my Dad's coat and zipped up tight. The four of us had walked in very freely with no confrontation at all and the drinking resumed. Once my Dad and his friends had found a secluded corner the zip was released a little so that I could have a little air.

Everyone was drinking and being very boisterous and the loud laughter had I supposed caught the attention of some of the security men who worked the door. Upon making eye contact with me and my little head popped out I imagine he couldn't believe what he was seeing and came bounding over in his strong East European accent demanded we leave immediately although laughing as he did so stating "he had seen it all now"!

I've been in every pub throughout the town and because I am a familiar figure everyone knows my name but I finally visited a night club also. How many dogs get to live the high life that I do them?

I am never to be found indoors as I am taken out on every occasion and on the few times I have been left in the home I would not be prepared to put up with that I would always have an escape plan hatched. The flats involved a buzzer type intercom access and I would be primed and on my toes better than Usain Bolt! The moment someone had been let in I would sprint for all my life was worth taking the stairs two and three at a time and out of that door at the bottom and to freedom with seconds to spare before it closed.

Adventure time for Stella. I could hear my name being called but it became more remote as I gained momentum and was now perhaps a hundred yards from the flat. I sat down to rest at the side of the canal and pondered what should I do for the rest of the day now I had all of this free time to myself. Build a raft, make a rope swing?

Whenever I had these outings it would always be a fun packed day. There would always be a lot of concerned and anxious faces when I did finally return but I used to laugh inwardly and think you should all sit down and watch a film called "Lassie come home". It was one of my all-time favourites and I had always managed to find my way back home.

Lassie had even managed to get herself a tattoo on one of her excursions and I promised myself I would watch out for a tattoo parlour myself on my travels. Why did humans think us dogs had a piss on every street corner that we passed. That was our own means of marking our route home. A sort of canine Satnav in a way.

But for now I crossed a few of the many bridges that crisscross any canal system and walk ways and found myself in the woods. Of course I would have been scared had it been night time but during the day I always found it to be a very pleasant experience. When I wasn't accompanied by humans the woods always seemed to have many more animals and birds in clear view, it was very much a back to nature experience for me and very enjoyable.

I would strut about like a tiger and if I heard any human voices I would conceal myself in the undergrowth quite covertly in case it was any of my Dad's search party. I would need to be wary of complete strangers coming across me because should they decide to take me home and they lived any great distance I would lose my Dad and I would never wish to do that. I simply want to have a little fun of my own.

It was after one of these escapades the decision was taken to chip me so that I could always be returned. A wise decision I suppose although I felt a little like a homing pigeon at the time. It wasn't as if I didn't know how to find my home and if my Dad wasn't there I knew to make for the local pub.

One time after a lengthy swim, I'd been missing for the best part of four hours, when I dripped my way into the pub and must have looked very comical. The barmaid rang my Dad to inform him I had just showed up at the pub I could tell by her face he was having an angry exchange. Of course I was going to show up at the pub because the entire bar staff gave me bones whenever I was in there. Now shape up and be a good girl and grab me one of them from the fridge and let me have a little gnaw on one of them before "Silly Bollox" walks in with a face like thunder.

There was only one time when these escapes backfired on me because I hadn't anticipated the weather when I had bolted and the whole area was blanketed in snow. It is the one season of the year I have difficulty with because I have to spring like a kangaroo through the snow and it is difficult to make much headway and it is very fatiguing. I was completely exhausted by the time I stopped to rest and didn't realise the snow was giving way and I found myself slipping down a small embankment and into a small stream that was flowing fast due to the recent thawing and excess water.

I was carried downstream and went under once or twice and became quite scared. I was carried for miles and found myself a long way from home. There was no way out of the water due to the brambles and nettles either side of the torrent and I imagined this was the end for me and I dreaded the outcome.

I was swept into a dam of sorts and did not know if animals or children had made this makeshift construction but all I know is it was a God send. I managed to crawl out and onto the bank and quickly gathered my senses but hadn't a clue where I was. All I knew was I was absolutely freezing and would have given anything to be back home safe and sound.

Nearby there was another council estate and as I watched one of the residents park their car I crawled underneath it for the sanctuary from the weather and also for warmth because the engine was still heated from its recent journey. It was here I was found the following morning and almost froze to death due to the elements worsening overnight and well below freezing.

A little girl spotted me under her Fathers car and they wrapped me in a blanket, the little girl saved my life and I will always be grateful!! I had my name on a tag, but no address, around my neck and I was taken indoors until inquiries could be made and my Father found.

I can honestly say that was the scariest experience and close to death encounter I am ever likely to have. I was a very lucky little girl and promised myself I would never do anything like this again as the heat from the living room fire, in the little girls home, defrosted me by the minute.

Once my Dad was contacted and showed up I expected him to be in a blind rage but once he realised I had appeared to have had a frightening ordeal his mood very much mellowed. He was very relieved to have found me and I didn't need no lecture if I was honest because I know already it would be a long time before I ever considered hatching an escape plane again.

My rescuers had told Dad how frozen I had been when I was found and instead of being as angry as I thought he would be he had gone out instead and purchased me a little parka coat with a fur hood on. I like to think he had done it with additional warmth for me in mind but maybe it was to restrict my movements also because it was difficult to run in that's for sure.

This is what I meant with my Dad no matter what I done wrong I would always come out the other end with a treat of sorts. Dad could never be angry with me for long, for sure he loved me. Yes I had found myself a keeper!! But I would need to behave a little more ladylike rather than the little bitch I was becoming.

CHAPTER 8

After this last little adventure it seemed to Dad I had returned with a limp and so he took me to the vets. He should have taken the time to read up about small terriers with our "limps" because we all have one. It's in our heads! It's a hereditary thing we all just bounce about with a hop and a little skip. When I was young I thought I had a disability myself until I seen others doing it.

When he told them about my recent escape and where I had been found and my escape from the stream everyone agreed we should take x-rays to be on the safe side and I was put to sleep for this to be done and chipped to my Dad's address while I was under.

I suppose it was for the best and the right decision but I had already decided to clip my own wings and to stop behaving so rashly. I had had a lucky escape and no-one knew that better than me.

In actual fact for the first time in my life I had even become fearful of even going swimming in water, it was a long while before I could muster the courage to enter the water again.

I had escaped a reprimand although I thought that would perhaps surface once the vet's bill arrived. Ouch! I sometimes slept in the small room by the letterbox so maybe I could hide the bill when it arrived until the dust settled.

When I was a little pup I used to tear things like that to shreds. Anything that came through the door, whoosh! I would dive on it like a cheetah does an antelope or any form of prey. But as I got older I had soon realised there was more fun to be had from keeping it all intact. Especially the official brown ones that Dad would choose to ignore and walk past them, leaving them untouched, time after time.

I would pretend I was being a good dog and pick them up with my mouth and drop them by his feet and retreat to my room having a little snigger while I waited for the usual mutterings and oaths regarding "bedroom tax" and "the bastard council".

He was constantly at loggerheads with the local council and I had begun to think it would be a wise move to get my name put on the rent book to safeguard my own future and security. Last thing I wanted was to find myself homeless.

I know how easily that could happen because I had just done a sleep out myself for the homeless teenagers in the town to raise money for Dad's favourite charity DOORWAY.

I listened to some of these kids stories and appreciated just how easily a person's situation can change for the worse and end up on the streets. Yes! I had decided my name needed to be on the rent book.

The problem was it always proved to be a little difficult accessing the local town hall because Dad could never be in attendance without causing a scene and I would guess by now we are both barred from the building and so I never get a chance to discuss my own wellbeing.

Sometimes it's not Dad who causes the outbursts but I have been with him long enough to quickly notice when his volcano is about to erupt and I just cover my eyes and ears and wait for the storm to pass. Oh no, a storms brewing!

A perfect example is when he had to attend the Justice Centre for Warwickshire in Nuneaton because he had to see his Victim

Support Worker. He proceeded to tie me to the railings outside the court house when a big burly security officer for the court house came over to tell Dad he couldn't leave me there. I looked from one face to another and then to the other.

Oh dear! This was going to be one of those confrontational episodes and I immediately placed my paws over my ears. "Why don't you fuck off and crack on with your duties"? The first salvo had been fired and in an instant it all became very heated with the officers challenge as to who did Dad think he was talking to. "Well there's only you I can see in front of me sweetheart"! Dad was on form and wasn't going to back down from this situation and brushed the officer aside as he entered the building.

Many people would consider I am to blame for all this commotion but none of you know my Dad and he is the one who creates the drama. He conducted his business but as a parting shot, before he untied me, he blew the officer a farewell kiss.

The end product of that day is Dad is barred from the local court building. It was suggested politely that he didn't come in again but in reality it means he is barred but now through his own actions. He no longer has a support worker and that leaves me to pick up the pieces and be his agony aunt.

He also got given several bouts of anger management where he had to lay on the floor and listen to whales and dolphins screeching and other piped music. Are you people for real? I live with this lunatic and can assure you that even SWIMMING with dolphins or riding hump back whales bareback would do little or nothing to placate this man's mental state so how you could possibly think calming music would do the trick is beyond me.

It wouldn't take them long to find out for themselves because when he showed up for one of his earlier sessions he had his arm and hand strapped up. I would have loved to have been a fly on the wall when he entered the room with the other angry patients.

He had knocked someone out the previous week, who had upset his sister and had been transferred to the University Hospital for emergency plastic surgery because of the injuries to his knuckles due to coming into contact with the victim's teeth.

You could honestly not make this shit up. Barred from the local courts and also showing up to anger management with a hand strapped up and broken and bust because of fighting.

I am one to talk though because the night he had been transferred to the other hospital for surgery I hadn't a clue where he was and it was the first night since we had been together that he had stayed out overnight and I done what all of us girls do in situations like this and smashed the flat to pieces.

The sight that greeted him once he came home about took his breath away as his mouth dropped open. Oh I had ragged the cushions about on previous occasions but this time I had made sure I had released all of the feathers and the end result would have been similar to a fox having been let loose in a chicken coop.

Who knows maybe I have anger issues of my own. I felt a little sorry when I saw the state of his hand but almost immediately thought "you silly twat" you better still be able to open my tins of food when I'm hungry.

Needless to say he was no longer welcome on his anger management course. I thought it was hilarious that he would have still expected a warm welcome.

The bloke's an out and out nut case who has had many spells in mental institutions and has a minimum of six or seven people live inside his head and I only know because I have met them all. When the council say to him that he is under occupying because he lives alone I laugh and think you haven't got a fucking clue because if anything this bloke is overcrowded.

He certainly is in his head!! L.O.L. It's a shame he can't get benefits for each of his personalities or we would be living in clover. I've met them all and most of them are harmless and they all seem to like little dogs so I just go with the flow and accept my situation.

He takes prescribed medication for his schizophrenia but as I say I don't care which one I wake to so long as he remembers that pets need feeding everything will be fine. I have checked all of his illnesses out on my smart phone so I know exactly what to expect in his moments of madness.

I would just sit and watch Paul O'Grady or other dog programmes on TV because I would always be in charge of the remote while Dad roamed from room to room talking to himself.

Reality would always resume at some point but I had long since accepted I was Dad's last line of defence! His full time carer and I would need to take the rough with the smooth!!

He was always seeing some care worker or other and he had now been passed on to some psychological nurse from the M.I.N.D group and how any of them thought they fully understood him was beyond me when they would only see him once a week.

I had been very unpredictable in my own behaviour had I not? So perhaps we were a match made in heaven and destined to be with each other. I'd definitely got my hands full and it was likely to be a full time job but one I was looking forward to.

The one certain thing throughout it all was there was never likely to be a dull moment and that's the way I preferred my life to be.

I didn't want a partner and Dad seemed to be the same so nothing or no-one was ever likely to come between us except him having a stay yet again in a mental asylum if he didn't stop his wayward behaviour.

I think we needed a holiday and each time he had thrown the glossy junk mail into the bin I would make a point of digging them out and placing them on the coffee table hoping he would take the hint.

I know Tenerife had been a disaster for him and he had sworn never to go to Spain again but he needed to remember I hadn't had a holiday myself recently. At least he had been abroad which was not possible for me but I would settle for a UK coastal area. Sort it out "Silly Bollox" we both need a break.

CHAPTER 9

There's only so much of the Coventry canal you can put up with and I was getting very bored with the tales of the riverbank. I know that canal tow path like the back of my hand and needed a change of scenery. I'd walked every inch of it barked at every barge and knew exactly where to find the swans every day to have a nose to nose with them and scatter the ducks sat on the embankment.

There's only so much fun to be had on a canal. The swimming side of it was always good except it got put on the banned list and that particular pastime was soon curtailed.

Since I'd stopped running away I'd had to settle for just going out with Dad and whatever he had bought to amuse me and when we went by the local running track I could not believe when he pulled out one of the scoop things and the accompanying tennis ball. When I chased the first ball I about collapsed in fits of laughter; did he actually know what a twat he looked? God! How I wished I had my phone with me for some video footage of this. I would send it viral L.O.L.

All of the activity was **all** well and good with me but it wasn't quite cutting it. Whenever I looked for the brochures on the coffee table they would be found in the bin yet again. I fully understood money was a little tight but if he put his mind to it a break would be possible and within our means.

It certainly would if he cut out what I called "the shelf antics"! How many times had I sat by all of their ankles and maybe I couldn't see what was actually on the shelf but it didn't take a fool to work it out what was going off and especially when the odd rolled up twenty pound note fell to the floor. I would always lay claim to them and sneak off to my stash which I hadn't checked for a while and was willing to bet there would be enough in there to cover a mini break.

One morning shortly after I had woken early and was sifting through the mail with the intention of hiding the mail I regarded as "bad post" because should he believe we were in debt up to our ears then we would be going nowhere when I heard voices at the door and a pair of eyes peeping through the door which I soon gathered belonged to one of the local constabulary.

I gave my fiercest growl but had long since accepted I had never mastered the art of sounding fearsome! My bite was okay and certainly did the trick but my bark left a lot to be desired. They did not go away for a long while because they were under the impression that if i was in the home then my Dad certainly was too because we were inseparable.

God knows what it was about but to be on the safe side I sprinted up the stairs to make sure that his "Glastonbury" tent hadn't been pitched again. He was fast asleep in the bedroom and I cursed him for sleeping as soundly as he was.

Would I ever be able to just live one day in peace around this fool when there wouldn't be any drama? Thankfully there was no tent in the building so I could relax a little although having said that there must have been some misdemeanour that Dad had been involved in simply through them being at the door.

He awoke due to my constant yapping and as he always did drew the curtains wide but upon spying the patrol car on the car park out the back he placed his index finger to his lips and indicated to be silent. Are you a complete fucking arsehole? It's me who has come up here to wake and forewarn you.

It acted as a kick up the arse for him and very much a big bonus for me. He spent the rest of the day amassing whatever funds he could muster. After packing an overnight case and a few extras we headed in the direction of the train station and I heard him order a return ticket to Dawlish Beach in Devon. I hadn't the heart to tell him I had by now overheard it was simply a routine enquiry and the police had knocked other neighbours on the landing also.

All I knew was I was on my way to the seaside and needed a kiss me quick hat and a bucket and spade. I had never been to the coast before and was very excited throughout the journey.

It took a few hours and changes of trains to complete the journey and once we arrived and I could just taste the freshness of the air in my lungs. I closed my eyes and relaxed but within a few seconds had to bolt towards the safe confines of the train station.

WTF was that? Jesus Christ! I had never been so scared. Something perhaps three times the size of me had just swooped in like a Golden

Eagle and tried to sweep me off my feet and I had visions of me being deposited in some cliff side nest for some smaller versions to devour me. I imagined that even the smaller ones would perhaps weigh the equivalent of what my Dad consumed in medication each week.

Forget the bucket and spade! My first purchase was going to be a saddle with weights at the side to keep me firmly on the ground. What was it with me and visiting other areas? It always seemed to be like the land of the giants and I was caught up in some science fiction movie. After a few days of shadow boxing and throwing the odd bark and chase in the direction of the seagulls they in turn had learnt to be just as scared of me.

Lots of people would stop to take photos of me squaring up to the gulls and I imagined it did look quite comical. I had chased pigeons before but this was a different level as I locked horns with the heavyweights of the feathered world.

I became more and more courageous and and each morning we left the hotel I would charge and scatter them and from being scared of one of them in the initial meeting I would gladly take three at a time on.

From my hotel room I could see the small beach at the side of the train station and the waves crashing up against the sea wall and I instantly liked it here and hoped Dad's "paranoia" meant we would remain on the run for weeks rather than days. The Blenhelm is what they called the hotel and that's exactly what it was to me (a palace) with its dog friendly approach. I was treated in a very special manner and exactly like any of the human guests and I would have every intention of staying here again.

Dad was nervous because he thought the police were looking for him and he was a fugitive and this feeling had made him very anxious and put him off his food. He had no appetite at all and I had read on the brochures that the breakfast had been given a five star rating. Uuum! Move out the way then Dad and pass me the cutlery while I confirm the five stars to be true.

I'm going to eat this and then have a little stroll down to the beach to pass my day. I'd already learnt my way around when I had done my toilet duties and I would strut about like I owned the area.

If the "fugitive" wanted to stay in the hotel room with his binoculars scanning the locals and the traffic that was entirely up to him but I wanted to run along the beach, feel the sand between my paws and have a few fights.

I enjoyed my period in this area better than I had any other area I had ever visited and I was a little sad when it was time to leave. I had even made friends with a few of the gulls by then and would share my crisps and sausage rolls with them and they would do the same with anything they had snatched from passer-by's.

When Dad had been ringing back home he had obviously gathered that he wasn't the object of police attention and the decision had been reached to return home within the next few days so I went and got myself yet another fridge magnet to remember the visit, bid farewell to the friends I had met and was sure I would visit this area again in the not too distant future.

I was becoming a frequent traveller by train and if it was possible for me to board any train unaccompanied I would readily travel the length and breadth of the country. But for now it was homeward bound again and I feel asleep with my head resting on Dad's upper thigh.

It was only a short break, but I had very much enjoyed it and I'm sure Dad did once he relaxed with the information that he actually wasn't on no wanted posters in Nuneaton. Fatten up the calf the prodigal son is returning home and I will have a plate of that as well.

CHAPTER 10

It was customary activity upon arrival back at the family home as Dad's friends arrived to gather all of the news regarding the holiday. All of the "usual suspects" and I knew instantly it was likely to be yet another long night as the first strains of the Stone Roses blasted out from the stereo.

God knows what the neighbours thought of the continued repetitive beats and I could now understand why the criminal justice bill had been introduced in the 1990's. It was on evenings such as this that I wished I could just gather my basket up and make for the nearby woods.

There was one track call "resurrection" which would always cause me to laugh because I had wondered through the living room at one time in the past and looked at this motley crew all comatose and let me assure you that not even 10,000 volts would not have "resurrected" this lot! The memory is a lasting one because I rather foolishly, had my first few tastes of Prosecco wine which seemed to taste nice at the time but as the old adage goes I literally really was sick as the proverbial dog and would not be going anywhere near that in the foreseeable future.

No doubt a letter from the council would be winging its way towards us regarding the loud and anti-social behaviour and to be truthful the other tenants had every right to be feeling aggrieved because it was becoming a regular occurrence. For Christs Sake! Even I couldn't sleep and was tempted to complain to the council myself.

It was as if this idiot thought that because of his expulsion from the court building he would never be able to be held to account for nothing. I'm sure he would have a very rude awakening shortly once he was led in to face the eviction process he had been threatened with on several occasions previously. Nobody would be singing "I want to be adored" then once we found ourselves homeless.

The following morning once the festivities had ceased Dad opened his mail and seemed excited about just the one letter in particular which involved the BBC Inside Out Programme that covers investigative journalism stories more than any other.

They were investigating historical brutality and cruelty committed by prison officers in the early 1970's and invited Dad to travel up to the North East of the country to give his account of what had taken place and the injuries he had occurred.

Upon eavesdropping on Dad's conversations I quickly gathered he had not had it particularly easy in the institution concerned and it made me very sad and tearful. But not for very long though!

I soon brushed sentiment aside! I was more concerned I was about to make my television debut because no way was he leaving me at home while I had a gilt edged opportunity to appear on national TV.

Where was my Filofax when I needed it? I would need my nails doing and obviously a full groom. I had long been using a parlour called Klassy K9's (because that's exactly what I was) and after each pampering session I would tear the pretty bow off that had been placed on my collar because I felt it wasn't befitting of a criminally minded dog such as myself. But on this occasion I would let it remain because I wished to create a lasting impression with the camera crew. This could be my big break!! Lassie, Tin Tin, Spit the Dog and Scooby Doo, they all had to start somewhere and this was going to be Stella Ginnelly's big break.

Plans were afoot and the BBC was picking up the bill to cover all travelling expenses and I sat by the front door and slept there for the next week. No-one was going anywhere without me also being in attendance.

My only fear was I had heard so many stories about the BBC and Jimmy Saville and I was a little girl with a pretty bow on so I hoped I would be safe up here on this visit. It was no good thinking I would be safe here because I was with my Dad because the last him he had been in this area he had been beaten senseless so I would have to keep my own wits about me.

Upon meeting the camera crew they had already been warned that the home office would not permit any filming to be done within close proximity to the institution and had been politely ushered away or faced the threat of the local constabulary.

The decision was reached to film in the farmer's fields close to the prison and I was a little angry because no one seemed to be considering me in all of this as we decamped to the muddy field. The cameras were set up and the interview commenced and by now my previously smart appearance had all but gone as I trudged through the tracts of mud and I looked a very sorry sight indeed!

At regular intervals I would gently tug at the bottom of the cameraman's trousers to attempt to attract his attention. Oi! You! Yes you! I'm down here! You need to move the camera in a downward motion.

All of these actions received not the least bit of acknowledgement and at one time I even got a gentle little shove with his foot and found myself in one of the field muddy puddles.

My dreams of stardom were short lived as by the time I had dusted myself down all of the equipment was being placed back in the van and it was handshakes all round and words of gratitude. You bastards! I not only hadn't made the small screen but I was absolutely filthy and would need to complete a return four hour train journey in this state.

I ripped the bow off in disgust at the first opportunity and cursed stardom. I was in a bad temper all the way home until I realised that these events what had taken place meant a lot to Dad and when the programme was finally aired he came across quite well and I was very much proud of him.

The matters have not yet been resolved although several of the officers are on police bail with the prospect of facing charges. In that era institutions were opened classed as "Short Sharp Shock" establishments but that does not give grown men a free rein to manhandle and brutalise young boys. Especially not to MY Dad you bullies! I hope justice will prevail in all of this but I would never hold out any hope for individuals taking on the establishment. Dad had me to comfort him anyway no matter what the outcome was.

I seemed to be spending quite a lot of time on trains recently and was becoming quite a little jet setter and I loved my life with my Dad. He took me absolutely everywhere and I was excited to hear that on the way back rather than complete the journey in one we would be breaking it up by visiting my Uncle Mick Fox and Auntie Caron Morton.

This was the life! Yippee! Although, I'd definitely got no intention of strolling the streets, but I would be content sitting safely with Mick and also in the knowledge that if he ordered a chinese takeaway half of it would be mine. Happy days indeed!

The more travel I had done my fears had lessened with each journey because I had become a little world wise I suppose and it took a lot to unnerve me.

My life had certainly changed for the better and I had very quickly become a celebrity in different counties up and down the country. All hail the Queen!! Although at the minute in time I looked far from Royalty whilst I was caked in mud from the farmer's field. It was Dad's constant apologies about my appearance that amused me because I had seen photographs of him as a little boy and it would have been possible to grow potatoes at the back of his ears he used to get that dirty. But I made for the bathroom and smartened myself up a little and listened to him and Dad recounting past memories to each other of their misspent youth while they both had a few cans.

I would enjoy these chance meetings because this was Dad's place of birth and you could always sense he was at his happiest when he was back in Yorkshire. I fell asleep, contentedly, amidst the fun and laughter of their anecdotes.

I had a feeling this would only be one of the many journeys I would make with my Dad though maybe I should get a little suitcase to put all of my destination labels on.

We spent a few days in Yorkshire before we resumed our journey and lots of new friends I had made on my previous visit had called around to see me bearing gifts. Space cakes had been placed on the side in the dining room and I had thought this was a term for some Yorkshire delicacy. Fortunately I had noticed that Dad had refused one and that had set alarm bells ringing because he has one of the sweetest tooth's of anyone I've ever met. I am usually a greedy dog and was tempted to wait my chance and smuggle one of the cakes under the dining table and eat it at my leisure. I was so glad I hadn't partaken in the freshly baked cakes. Train travel was one thing!! Space travel seemed a completely different kettle of fish and I didn't fancy orbiting Micks Kitchen.

Yet again farewells and cuddles and pats were exchanged and with heavy hearts we made our departures. I could tell Dad was loathe to leave, I myself had begun to love this area and its people like it was my own.

We would need to travel to Leeds to make our connection for the Midlands and at each train station I would take my time completing my toilet duties in the hope that we would miss our connection and therefore delay our arrival in Nuneaton.

I would never be in a rush to get home because I would love these outings with just me and Dad and each other for company. He was the one for me; I had finally met a keeper.

Once we arrived in Nuneaton I knew it would always be the same and there would be something or someone that would stress Dad and change the whole mood. He had in actual fact written a bestselling book called NEVER A DULL MOMENT and that about summed the area up perfectly.

The problem was all the untoward activity seemed to take place around us and the only quality time either of us got was on these train journeys. It was the life I had chosen so I would need to take it all with a pinch of salt. I certainly wouldn't want to go back to my previous life and I was here now and for the long haul. Till death us do part so to speak although me and this mad little fucker I called Dad had many more miles on the clock yet.

I have recently had my twelfth birthday and although that may seem a lot in dog years I am still in excellent shape and fit as a fiddle. When you're doing ten miles a day on foot with a Dad like mine who can't sit still I definitely have no need for a treadmill or an exercise bike. I'm afraid me and "Silly Bollox" will be regular features in this town for many more years yet.

We arrived back safely late evening which gave us time to have a good night's sleep. Should there be any problems they can be faced in the morning.

CHAPTER 11

Over the next few days after arriving back I was having great difficulty doing my number two toilet duties and Dad must have asked other people about what it could possibly be and had been given instructions what to do. But I was not aware of this! When I had been picked up to deposit in my recently ran bath I thought no more of it than it was my regular bath time and practically skipped into the bathroom ready for a good splash about.

I did think it a little strange when I noticed Dad had a rubber glove on his hand and he began to lubricate two of the fingers. As he made contact with my rear area I sprinted to the furthest end of the bath.

OMG!!! WTF!!! Whoa mister! A bridge too far. I knew we were close but this was insane. Did he just try to have foreplay with me?

He vanished from the bathroom rather sheepishly and I would need to clamber out of the bath by myself. It was a while before I ventured down the stairs to the living room as I tried to take stock of what had just taken place. I found Dad hiding behind a newspaper which I was thankful for because neither of us could make eye contact with each other for the remainder of the evening. I felt violated!!

I couldn't come to terms with what happened until I heard Dad talking to one of his friends and realised he was simple trying to release some of my glands that blocked up and apparently it was a common practise with this problem and especially the small breed of terriers. The incident was never mentioned again and at least I now knew Dad was just as embarrassed as I was.

He found out at a later date that my own dog parlour dealt with this self-same problem when requested to do so. Needless to say I never seen the rubber glove put in an appearance again and any of my plumbing problems would be resolved down the parlour. Girl on girl action! Who knows if I swung that way or not! The one thing I did know is I had put a NO ENTRY sign at the top of me tail in clear view for my Dad to see.

No way would that be happening again, you could be sure of that. I was glad I hadn't notified social services at the time of the incident and it turned out there is a perfectly innocent explanation for Dad's actions.

I curse myself for doubting him because he always looked after me to the best of his capabilities. Sometimes a little too much. I certainly didn't dare let him see me scratch for any great length of time or he would go into overdrive he was that obsessive with his cleaning disorder.

Domestos bleach, disinfectant, big dom, Mr Sheen or any amount of detergents would put in an appearance and not only would all of my bedding be washed and pegged out on the line but me also with a peg holding each of my ears onto the line while I dried in the sun.

Dogs get fleas! I wanted to scream it at him but I suppose it was my own fault and I should have only scratched in a room where he wasn't present. Never mind! At least I could be thankful I never got thrown in the washing machine although I bet it crossed his mind on a few occasions. I would be doused with every medication known to man and I would have every sympathy with the few fleas that were comfortably snug at the at the back of one of my ears because their demise would have seemed like chemical warfare to them.

I would always be quite easily the cleanest dog on the estate and I would guess word had been passed around in the flea world to give me a wide berth and bed down on any dog except me because bazooka Joe (my Dad) would exterminate them like no extermination ever.

I seemed to live in the bath and was always in soppy suds up to my neck and perhaps it might be a good idea to get me a hot tub when Christmas came around next.

I couldn't win because I was always getting told off for moulting on the carpet. I used to think it was more his fault than mine for having a dark brown coloured carpet and I couldn't help the fact I was snow white could I now? Perhaps I wouldn't have lost as much fur if he didn't constantly be dipping me in all of these chemical based shampoos every two minutes.

Everywhere I walked I would smell like a hospital ward and other passing dogs would avoid me. It any of these passing dogs fleas jumped onto me by the time the next dog passed by they would jump right off again onto that one instead. I imagined them choking like on CS gas as they vacated my body with or without any parachutes.

I couldn't complain I suppose because I had known times when Dad had paid for me a full groom rather than pay for a week's shopping from Iceland. I had been put before his provisions and on more than one occasion I might add.

I found that to be an absolutely amazing gesture because at this time my Dad also needed to use the food bank due to government sanctions placed upon him. I had watched from a distance and found it all to be very unfair because Dad had paid many contributions whilst he worked and now they seemed hell bent on destroying him now he had fell on hard times.

The food bank was a joke really and many people believe it is a regular practise when in actual fact recipients can only use it on three occasions throughout the year and even then only be allocated emergency provisions to cover a three day period. Not exactly the banquets of kings that everyone is under the impression exists is it? When Dad used them the very first time he came home very much embarrassed and made the decision to not use them again and told many people that he would rather starve.

I wouldn't exactly be the happiest dog in the world neither because once I stuck my snout in the bags to have a sniff about it was very much basic provisions of rice and pasta and not even a single item for a pet.

It was going to leave me very much on a wing and a prayer because hadn't I just recently been put on a weight watchers diet so I wouldn't be seeing much of the fucking pasta unless I found some way to fiddle the bathroom scales.

Dad had become good friends with Ken Loach because of the hardship he was going through and even though the film producer must have been very busy man he always finds time to respond to my Dad's messages and I for one am thankful we have him in our corner because the situation for everyone lately is worsening by the day.

Dad and I slept out rough recently to raise funds for the homeless teenagers and we are always in one charity event or another and it seems that with most of us our only hope of survival is to help each other and I always get myself involved and its every dogs duty to do so and raise awareness.

The way things were panning out here it wouldn't be too long before the council tried to force us out. Where did they think we were going to go, were we expected to build a log cabin out in the woods and live from the land.

I was never a political dog before I came to live with my Dad but I soon appreciated the difficulties that were being imposed on people with no consideration for the people concerned.

And I was thankful for the fact that he chooses whatever little money my Dad had to eke out a very poor existence I would always be placed at the top of his list. I'd surely got myself one of the best dog owners in the whole of the town.

I would sit outside of the Town Hall in Nuneaton with a Gregg's sausage roll and a cup of water every Monday morning without fail. It became a ritual! I would be tied loosely around one of the big marble pillars and even though it seemed a safe distance it wouldn't take that long before I could hear Dad ranting and raving. He must have known in his heart that no amount of confrontation was going to change the situation and I think he just showed up each Monday out of devilment and to be disruptive. He was often threatened with the police and would make himself scarce at these times and exit the building.

Apart from the commotion I would look forward to the Monday morning stroll through the park to the town because I was guaranteed my little treat while I waited for Dad to finish his outburst.

For some strange reason I was not welcome in the building. Perhaps the Mayor didn't like dogs! Who knows! It mattered little or nothing to me because I had no inclination to meet the Mayor anyway.

Our routine never varied a little rant and rave there culminating in a visit to Doorway to check on the wellbeing of the homeless teenagers. Doorway is the charity that represents them and Dad has long since adopted it as his favourite charity because he was homeless and on the streets himself as a small child of fourteen years of age

While I went from place to place with my Dad I would witness just how unfortunate some people were including him. Although he was poor he would share what little he had with anyone at all who was in need. Every single day of the week he would put an appeal out through social media inviting anybody round for a meal and that was irrespective of whether he knew them or not.

I found this arrangement to be very satisfactory because on the days when any guests would arrive then for sure my diet would go out of the window completely. If it was just myself and Dad in the flat he would make sure my regime was stuck to rigidly. But I would rub my paws in glee when we had visitors because I would sit so close to them while they ate I could actually feel the heat form the gravy on my chin. Nobody could even begin to look at my angelic little face without leaving at least a few scraps and Dad would often overlook how much I was eating.

Oh I know every trick in the book! Why the fuck should I be counting the calories while the rest of you are gorging a minimum of three times a day. I would laugh at times when I was reprimanded for chewing up the odd tennis ball. Hadn't the daft twat stopped to realise I was perhaps starving if I had ever gone three or four day without additional food.

At other times I probably weighed more than some of the drug consignments he delivered but it mattered not one jot to me. Why in actual fact did I need to be fit??? I thought we had decided long ago I wasn't cut out to be hunting or chasing rabbits so it was the good life I intended for myself and if that meant lots of food then by all means pass me a knife and fork.

I wished he would just focus on his own issues and leave me alone. If he wanted a tougher regime for himself then feel free by all means to give yourself a little rehab. It certainly wasn't on my agenda and anyway rehabs for quitters.

CHAPTER 12

Dad was becoming quite a local celebrity due to both of his books becoming best sellers. WELLIES AND WARDERS and the sequel NEVER A DULL MOMENT had both done really well and gone to the top of their category on AMAZON and to this day are still available for purchase.

He had been voted speaker of the year at the local Women's Institute and had now been invited to appear on the Vic Minett show on BBC Radio Coventry and Warwickshire so the limelight beckoned a little for him but I wouldn't be making the mistake again of poncing and pruning myself for the BBC and in actual fact I even let him go by himself.

He was doing quite well in my opinion because I kid you not, here was a man who needed to consume a wheelbarrow full of medication each week simply to focus on everyday duties and behave in a normal manner. I was the one who had to live on the frontline with him on the days when the blinds would remain closed even though it was blazing sunshine outside. All means of communication would be shut down and contact with the outside world would be non-existent during these periods.

His psychiatrist would have "Team Meetings" to discuss his progress and I would laugh inwardly at these times in my opinion they had only managed to trace perhaps two of his personalities. Oh trust me there were many more they hadn't even had the pleasure of meeting. But I had!

He could conduct himself in an orderly manner, to all intents and purpose, when he needed to but when he hit the other end of the spectrum his behaviour could be very challenging to say the least. But the good days outweighed the bad so I was happy to accept the situation as I waved him off to his Radio interview. He came back in a very elated mood so I presumed it had all gone well and would enhance book sales.

Not long after the fraud squad from the Department of Work and Pensions had him in for an interview regarding any profit margin they deemed he was making. Jesus Christ! Did they believe he had suddenly become J. K. Rowling overnight because the reality was we were both struggling on a daily basis still?

It would be wise at this moment to forewarn any budding author that any form of publication online represents limited Royalties and the rewards are pennies rather than pounds. It really is a case of swimming amongst sharks and the benefits are stacked in favour of whichever multinational company you choose to do business with.

We would receive Royalties at the end of each month but only very minimal. I would always know when they had arrived because I would suddenly be the proud owner of yet another new collar or an additional treat. At least he had received the acclaim that went with the achievement of writing two best-selling books which I suppose gave him every reason to feel proud.

His eyesight, by now, was beginning to fail him and he would struggle to write for any great length of time and it was with this in mind I had taken the decision to put pen to paper and write my own book and then we could both retire gracefully on the proceeds. It wouldn't exactly be in the lap of luxury but as long as we could have a little comfort in our lives we would get by because this life on benefits is a continual struggle.

Due to Dad being in the limelight the D.W.P had taken a closer look at his situation and invited him in for an Independent Medical Review Board over in Birmingham. Did these experts really believe he could switch his moods on and off like a kettle? I am his full time Carer and I should have been able to attend but that was not possible it seemed.

So off he went on what he thought was some sort of adventure and he didn't even begin to understand the enormity of the interview. He certainly would once the letter with the "expert" medical opinion dropped through the letterbox within a few weeks. He exploded with the discovery that his benefits were about to be reduced even further. I had never seen him in such a rage like this for quite a while.

I waited while he left the room and read the contents of the letter and the content appeared to suggest that because he could place his hands on his head or bend down and touch his toes then he wasn't quite as mentally ill as he was first diagnosed. I, myself was staggered and went to send an e-mail in protest only to discover my smart phone had obviously been reported stolen and was now blocked. Not the best start to the day for either of us it seemed. How could they seriously determine that he wasn't mentally ill??

They would need to be in attendance when he was roaming about the flat naked and talking in foreign tongues. I could well remember one recent incident when he had thrown the TV out of the front window with no thought of the safety of other people walking below obviously believing himself to be a member of some fictitious rock and roll band. This would need a second opinion for sure because any further hardship would begin to affect my own well-being. It seemed life was to be one constant struggle to exist with all of these government sanctions.

Would I soon be required to yet again go out shoplifting or perhaps the "Glastonbury" tent would need to be pitched again to find an alternative source of income. Dad seemed to be a defeated man. He looked more and more like a boxer on the ropes knowing he was just the one final punch away from hitting the canvas.

He was at a loss as to what to do and I could see the despair etched all over his face. Where possible he spent his whole life showing acts of kindness even to complete strangers and did not deserve to be treated in this manner. I worried for his health more than at any other time because he gave the impression that his final nail had been placed in his coffin.

There seemed no way to lighten his mood and I thought it unwise to attempt to elevate his mood by doing handstands and walking on my paws in front of him or juggling a few tennis balls.

I knew he had registered an appeal and it would be a case of playing the waiting game now. Living with my Dad though had taught me form an early age that people don't necessarily which to become embroiled in crime it comes about through the circumstances of situations like the one above.

He was on a short fuse for the next few days and I got the blame for just about everything. It was "allegedly" me to blame for the excessive number of socks he seemed to have lost and I must have been playing with them and had chewed them up. UUUM! I don't fucking think so mister! It hadn't crossed his mind to check the pipes within the washing machine. No! He had made his mind up and I was to be the scapegoat. Whilst he discussed the sock situation with his friend and also convinced him I was the culprit his friend suggested that he got me toys to play with and to get my teeth into instead. For fucks sake! For the last bleeding time, I don't know anything about his stupid socks!

His friend suggested that if he got me a few rabbit toys to play with it may possibly refresh my memory about just what my natural hunting instincts were. What on earth were this pair rambling on about? I checked in the ashtray to make sure they hadn't been smoking strange substances.

Later that evening once Dad had gone to bed I went onto his laptop and typed in RABBIT TOY and I about fell off the settee. OMFG!!! What come up was some seductive picture of some lady called Ann Summers and my eyes about popped out of my sockets. Dad's friend had said I should play with rabbits and this had come up. I was in total shock! Did this mean the dreaded rubber glove would be putting in an appearance at bath times again? I raced to the kitchen and disposed of every glove in there depositing them in the refuse bin as I let my imagination run away with me.

I would be safer right now living with Jimmy Saville and Gary Glitter instead of my Dad and his friend. I had a very restless night's sleep and had nightmare visions of me being turned into a sex slave to bring extra income into the house.

Maybe the "Glastonbury" tent was about to be turned into a red light district and other dogs would be brought to the premises. How had my life come to this I thought as I mistakenly dreamed up many different scenarios? I spent the rest of the evening very much on edge and sleep would not come easily until I took one of Dad's Zopiclone tablets from his first aid drawer.

I would finally conclude that because I was spending so much time in the company of a paranoid schizophrenic that I was beginning to become one myself. I immediately cancelled the online order I had placed for racy lingerie as I convinced myself I had read the situation completely wrong. Instead I replaced the order with one for a dozen pair of sport socks with Dad in mind to at least take the odd sock complaint right out of the equation.

Everyone's stress levels within the home had hit the roof including my own! Dad had all of these professionals in his corner in respect of his disturbed frame of mind and yet always appeared to be fighting his battles singlehandedly. He really was mentally ill!

Why couldn't people understand that and why wouldn't he be, considering all he had endured throughout his life? His life had been very brutal and I knew this because I had read his books at times during the night when I had a little free time. I was absolutely amazed that he had survived to the extent he had if I was truthfully. Many other given the same set of circumstances would have drowned and sank without a trace. He had been in many psychiatric hospitals and had always been treated for anxiety and depression and I would have been staggered had he not been.

He was a good strong individual and upon completion of his books I had a different insight into his nature and had even more reason to feel proud he was my Dad.

We both needed each other and my happiest memories are when he is falling asleep on the settee and I jump up on to his chest and rest my head on his shoulder to also go to sleep and as he nods off he proclaims "we are a team Stella". No other words than those five give me greater comfort and if I can even give Dad a fraction of that comfort in return then I will be a happy dog. Yes indeed! We definitely are a team!

CHAPTER 13

I imagined we would never be apart and only one situation ever tested that declaration. We were both headed towards the local shops one day and I had done my customary "number two" and as was the norm Dad picked it up and strolled onwards with the bag and contents in his hand. I had noticed a police care pass and return in the same direction albeit at a slower pace as if circling us like a shark. Suddenly the car pulled alongside one of the officers jumped out and grabbed Dad by the throat and put him up the wall demanding to know "what's in the bag?"

This seemed to in some way involve me due to the actual contents so I did what any "brave" dog would have done in the circumstances. I RAN for the hills or the woods in my case. I was off like a lightning bolt! I wasn't to know that Dad had previous form many years ago for delivering packages throughout the estate.

I would certainly like to have been there when the officer actually placed his hand in the bag and making contact with what he believed to be a shipment of illicit drugs. But because I was unaware of Dad's past I once again let my imagination run wild thinking I had committed some crime myself because of the interest in the bag.

I dug a little hole and covered myself in leaves before the helicopter could be scrambled.

No way could I deal with the hardship of a prison sentence. My mind raced!

Dad had a big family throughout the state and I knew plenty about what they got up to and if push came to shove I was sure I could come to some deal with the police. I had heard of "The Omerta" the code of silence but at this moment in time I wasn't sure I could adhere to it. Would I need to go on a witness protection programme?

What a predicament to find myself in and it I could get myself out of this I would solemnly swear to never "dump" on a public highway again. Wouldn't it have been funny though if the two officers concerned had sent the two tiny turds off to forensics for confirmation of what the substance was?

By now I thought a full dragnet was in force searching for me and I remained hidden for the rest of the day. I had rolled and rolled in a black mud hole to camouflage my appearance and conceal my white fur coat.

It was late evening when I returned to the home and I watched from the safe confines of the trees until I realised that there was my Dad having a cigarette out on the landing. I ran from my place of refuge and barked and barked up to the landing and although Dad looked over once or twice he simply resumed what he had been doing previously.

Oi! Down here you silly twat! I thought as I barked yet again. Little realising I had excelled myself this time and was the blackest I have ever been.

I got away without much of a lecture this time because he was pleased to see me. Not that pleased though that I was welcomed into the flat immediately. I was made to wait on the landing while the familiar deed of filling the bath was put in place. Mr Sheen may clean umpteen things clean BUT it wouldn't have even touched the surface on this particular evening.

It was fortunate that I had many expensive dog shampoo's because no dog ever spent as much time in the bath as I did. I looked at the toilet, whilst I was in the bath, and decided I may need to learn to use that to prevent any further police attention until I realised later I had read the situation wrong entirely yet again!

It was nice to see that the police can actually respond to what they believe to be a crime as quickly as they did because people had begun to lose faith in them. Congratulations to them on their exploits on that day L.O.L.

I know what Dad is like and he would have milked the one up man-ship from that day to the maximum; and by doing so not doing himself any favours.

That became clear within a very short period of time as the door came crashing in with splintered wood going in all directions. It wasn't the first time the door had been battered in and I thought it might be an idea to actually leave the door off and employ a porter. The place was fast becoming a hotel anyway so why not take that final leap and employ a porter to carry luggage in and out.

Meanwhile here were the customary big burly officers in uniform for intimidation purposes I supposed as I walked past them, yawning and made for my food bowl, had a quick snack and returned to my bed. They had done this before and when would they ever learn that they would never find any incriminating evidence in here?

The door had been weakened on a previous visit and now due to this further intrusion it was certainly on its last legs but if Dad used his head that would come in handy during the winter months as a sledge for me and him to slide down the steep incline outside the Donnithorne Hill.

I'd no doubt it had been a good sturdy door at one time but recently it had as many police boot prints as it did brush strokes. On closer inspection I wouldn't be surprised if it even had the odd bullet hole in it.

Police had become common place in my life and I became that familiar with some of them that we were even on first name terms. Dad was a wise old owl by now and had long since taken the decision to turn his life around anyway and the quicker the police realise that the better. Everyone else could see that he had reformed so why couldn't they? He was a man of standing lately and had even been voted an outstanding member of his community and his award still sits proudly on the shelf.

It's nice that he gets acknowledged now for all of the right reason and why not? He is involved in assisting many of the town charities by way of fund raising or whatever he feels is beneficial. He is in touch on a weekly basis with a good friend of his whom over the years has raised in excess of £250,000 for various good causes.

A certain Charles Bronson Salvador who in my Dad's eyes is enduring one of the biggest injustices this country has known. In no way should this man still be held in solitary confinement after 35 years. He is a good natured man who displays acts of kindness on a daily basis. He posts my Dad pieces of art only with helping people on his mind and each piece retails at auction for fees of £800 and upwards.

This man is completely reformed and should be released at the earliest opportunity and given the chance to have a progressive future by way of his art. Dad has paintings of his own on the wall from Charlie and although I find them to be a little bit abstract Dad loves them. That's possibly because of all the time he spent in solitary himself he identifies with Charlie in many ways.

FREE THE ARTIST SALVADOR

There is a petition with that heading online and Dad encourages everyone to sign it. Charlie is a changed man and so is my Dad.

Only recently he attended a function where the Mayor and Mayoress were on their feet applauding him for his deeds throughout the estate. All a bit fucking surreal if you ask me; but he hadn't thrown a TV out of the window for a while, so I was happy to put up with the "New Dad" no matter what it had brought about. About fucking time to be fair!

He had spent eleven years in a lot of different prisons' so let's be right he hadn't been the most successful criminal the country had ever known.

Time had passed him by and it was all about Cyber Crime now and that would have been like a maze to this arsehole who barely knows how to even switch a laptop on. But I loved him for all his faults. He had opened his door to me when I was very much a problem child and we seemed a perfect match who had lots of fun.

I doubted the police would be paying many more visits to our address and so we could replace the front door knowing it would remain intact for many years now. As stated previously the old door will be a good accessory to have once the snow arrives. Out of all bad comes good hey!

I couldn't understand why the police would want to harass us anyway because Dad was now officially recognised as a saint and the biggest crime I had committed was I had cleared the area of squirrels be they red or grey. I just liked chasing other wildlife and only once or twice have I caused alarm by doing so.

Dad was talking to a friend by the dole office next to the park for what seemed like an eternity and I was bored so resorted to my favourite past time and I wouldn't say I dived in with a splash because that would have alerted Dad. I simply slid in like a crocodile and inched my way to where all of the parents were feeding the ducks with their small children. The ducks scattered. The children screams echoed around the park so I thought I had better come out and let them see it wasn't exactly the Loch Ness Monster. I splodged through the mud on the embankment to let them see I was even small than Tom Thumb. "It's only me" I tried to explain to them but it didn't placate them any.

Get here! Now! Shouted the mad one who is my Dad and I made my way towards him black from the waist down and white from the waist up. Like some sort of zebra and I had to walk around town like that all day which didn't please him none neither. Oh Dad! Shut the fuck up and grab me an ice-cream. There's Tony's van by the fountain.

Don't go on and on, get your shoes and socks off and have a wade yourself. Or can you not do that now you are this outstanding member of the community. Get a grip and have a little fun; or if you insist on being serious get yourself in that Town Hall and get my fucking name put on the rent book. Maybe you could beat the bedroom tax saying I'm living with you. Just a thought!!

CHAPTER 14

Whilst we walked through town one of them small booths had been set up with men in uniform. You've got to have seen them before. An Army Careers Unit. One of the soldiers was laughing at Dad saying "Hey up mate! Your dog looks as if it's just completed one of our assault courses" while he laughed raucously.

Excuse me I thought, but I would obviously piss your so called gruelling course and for a moment it set me thinking of joining the Army. I quite fancied the idea of me parachuting behind enemy lines. I soon dismissed the idea because I was never such a clever dog in the summer with regard to the heat and it wouldn't do me any favours getting posted to the Middle East. I did think I would make a good little soldier and I was quite fit for my age.

We ambled around town for a while and Dad did all of his charity duties as he did religiously each time we were close by. I knew I was in the bad books because of how dirty I had got in the park so I did what I always did at these times and raced towards the fountain by the bronze statue to clean myself up a little but I dived in to an empty base because all of the water had been drained and the usual cascade of water was nowhere to be seen.

Had the council yet again showed us a cruel side to their nature because I had swam in this same fountain on hundreds of previous visits to the town centre although on reflection I now recalled Dad being rebuked on the last visit?

Apparently I had been observed slipping into my bikini at the side of the water and within seconds of me making my first splash two Community Constables had appeared and told Dad it wasn't allowed. A heated debated followed but to save any further trouble I had got dressed and tugged at the bottom of Dad's jeans motioning to him that we should leave and abide by whatever by law they were going to invoke on us.

But for them to have now taken the decision to drain the system seemed a little pathetic to say the least. I was sure I wasn't the only dog that used the fountain to cool down on a hot summer's day or any other days come to that.

Dad left me with a few of his friends and went to the local hardware shop while I sat outside one of the local public houses. When he returned he had a mountain of wood under his arm and a bag of odd bits and bats and told his friends he had "a good surprise for Stella when he got home". I won't lie I was very intrigued and could not wait to return home. He sat outside the pub exchanging funny anecdotes with his friends and it seemed a really amiable gathering and on any other day I would be more than content to fall asleep at his feet and while away the rest of the day. But the surprised had captured my attention and I began to play up a little and appear restless to prompt him to make his departure.

Upon arrival back home he disappeared under the stairs, closing the door behind him, and proceeded to bang, clatter and drill his way through the next hour. I was becoming anxious and somehow convinced myself I was about to become yet another PRISONER 1314 BRONSON and I was about to be held in a solitary cage and be on lockdown because of my continual naughty behaviour. I would only ever be let out again if I had five people in attendance; my Dad and four of his mates as the "guards".

I was very sad faced and woeful because I knew I had brought this on myself. When dad finally resurfaced and commanded that I come to have a look I did so albeit with a heavy heart. I genuinely thought I was going to be in solitary confinement for however long Dad thought it was likely to take to curb my behaviour. I entered the area with my tail between my legs fearing the worst but to my sheer delight he had been erecting wooden shelving accompanied by many different little dog statuettes of Jack Russell's and a sort of disco light to illuminate the area.

This is exactly what I keep telling you all? Hadn't I got the best owner in the world? I almost cried with relief that I wasn't about to be caged for the rest of my days. I suppose he realised that I missed my children and he wanted to make my setting as comfortable as possible.

He was the same in the living room and surrounded by photographs of his missing children I witnessed on a regular basis the pain and grief this caused him. We both had a different set of circumstances but in a strange sort of way the same outcome. I had been separated from mine for whatever reason whereas he had been unfortunate enough to meet one of those many women who feel they are god-like enough to tell lies and deny the Father the love of his children.

I loved my new room but more than that I absolutely adored my new Dad. It seemed like it had taken an eternity to find a man such as this but found him I had and from here on in I knew we would now become inseparable. Even my ornaments weren't cheap and very life like in respect of the Jack Russell breed. I was glad he had purchased the disco light because at this moment in time I was definitely in the mood to dance although I would need to be careful for fear of breaking any of my recently acquired ornamental "puppies".

I woke in the morning in a very happy mood and to add to my delight discovered we would be attending a party at the weekend at my Dad's sister's home. I had been promised to be taken to a proper festival for a long time now but as of yet it still hadn't happened but it was on the horizon this coming weekend and I had heard all about his sister Susan and her boyfriend Luke's mini festivals on the back garden.

I promised to myself that I needed to behave accordingly for the remainder of the week and not ruin my chance of attending. It was quite easy to not get under Dad's feet because I would be very busy admiring my little room and putting a few additions of my own in there to further brighten it up and make it even more homely.

I had taken one of Charlie Bronson's postcards that Dad had received and found it a prominent spot because I liked Charlie's face smiling sown on me as it made me feel safe. I also had a few of my favourite canine celebrity photos on display and especially Toto from the Wizard of Oz who was my favourite little dog of all time.

The weekend approached and half of the estate would be up there. My Dad really loved his sister Susan and they had both been together at Glastonbury when they discovered their Mum had died. They both had a very special bond with each other and had been to many festivals together. Sue had been to India a few times and the lay out of her home suggested exactly that and she was very much what could loosely be described as a peace loving hippy.

Once we arrived and were greeted warmly and I was like a dog with two tails and didn't know where to feast my eyes first. I lost Dad at the first chance I could and set about exploring from room to room just being naturally curious and in an upstairs room I came across the most relaxing area you were ever likely to see with statues of Buddha in each corner and it turned out this was the meditation room to do yoga. I practised a few positions myself while I was I there and out of view because I knew I wouldn't be missed just yet.

By now I'd guess that Dad would be that much into the swing of things that I doubted he would even recall that he had even brought me. Oh I had a free rein and I was certainly going to make the most of it as I came across people with lots of multi coloured beads and clothes and a few doing Crystal Stone Healing. Yes for sure this was my sort of party and had a very mystical feel to it.

When I ventured out onto the large sprawling garden a few tents and Indian Tipis were in place and a stone circle fire with perhaps half a dozen people with hand craved TomTom drums and all of them getting a continued beat and rhythm going which was very pleasant to the ear. This was all very tribal and I doubted very much we would be listening to any of the Stone Roses in this setting.

I could see Dad with a few of his friends at the top of the garden and as I came close enough to hear them giggling and the M.D.M.A. kept getting mentioned I took a few steps back. Oh dear! A pure strain of ecstasy was likely to give this odd job lot a more than interesting night and even though I had become a little thirsty by now my own personal alarm bells made me wary of drinking anything that was in the cups and glasses scattered about. I don't think I was scared at the possibility of being date raped. I just wanted to make sure I enjoyed my first party at Sue's and would rather not be drugged to the eyeballs and spoil the occasion. Glancing across at the state of Dad and his friends it was appearing to be a wise decision.

I went and introduced myself to just about everyone throughout the house and it was the friendliest company I had ever come across.

At some stage of the evening I ventured down the garden to the tented area and I would like to tell you that I'd popped inside one of them to see what mystical objects I might find but unfortunately hunger got the best of me and I was foraging for food.

The people who owned the tents had already been given clearance to stay overnight and I had guessed right about provisions as I came across a few packets of biscuits and snacks and made myself comfortable as I set about putting a big hole in the contents.

The weather had taken a little turn for the worst. Not exactly a heavy downpour! Only a slight drizzle but enough rain for the owners of the tent to take the decision to zip up the tents therefore ensuring their contents remained dry. This by now included Yours Truly as I found myself locked within the tent. No possible way out and as loud as I barked or yapped I could not be heard because by now everyone had gathered around the camp fire and the incessant pounding of the drums would drown out any noise I could possibly make.

It soon became clear that I was stuck in here for the foreseeable future and it wasn't the sort of night I had expected but would accept my fate like a good dog. I settled down for the night comfortable in the knowledge I had a carrier bag full of snacks to bring a little comfort to my predicament. It would prove to be a long night, I rummaged deeper and deeper into the bag to try and find something a little meatier until the realisation set in that I was, in actual fact, surrounded by lots of vegetarians'. Go to sleep Stella! You've fucked it up again!

Dad had apparently searched and searched for a few hours I had been told later but the last time I had seen him I doubt he could have even located one of his own brain cells let alone me and to rub salt in my wounds he had even given up on me as a lost cause and gone home without me. Not the most notable memory of my first mini festival. But I had enjoyed it and would definitely be putting in an appearance again. Just not zipped up inside a fucking tent!

CHAPTER 15

I would never be worried about getting lost and not finding my way home anymore because I had a minimum of two to three chips in the back of my neck. The problem was one or more may have been to a different address than the one I was residing at now. On reflection it may have been these bleeding things that made me continually scratch in that area. I had been shown the door at that many homes that if one of these chips had come up with one of them as the registry address I pictured everyone diving behind the settee and hurriedly closing the blinds. I hadn't exactly been everyone's favourite pet when I was younger.

I was only little and it might be a good idea for Dad to introduce a small cat flap for me to come and go as I pleased. I would never ever become a regular stray dog because no matter which ever circumstances came about nothing would ever prevent me from finding my way home. I would never let that happen because I would miss my home too much. I would swim rapids and run across hot coals to get back to my Dad.

I bet he wished he had got a cat flap on the occasion his granddaughter and her friends stayed for the night. They had got out of their own beds and attempted to leave the flat. I knew they were being naughty and growled at them from the room under the stairs but they took no notice. My barking became louder and woke him up but not before the teenagers had snapped the key inside of the lock and we were now, all of us, confined to the flat with no means of escape.

It was suggested that I could be lowered down on knotted sheets to raise the alarm but he was definitely off his rocker if he thought I was risking my safety from a first floor flat. Here we go again yet more fucking drama. If he hadn't already had the copy right for the title NEVER A

DULL MOMENT, I would seriously have considered it for the title of my own book.

He chastised them all and sent them back their beds and now the fun really began. He contacted one of the neighbours to pour milk through the letter box using a funnel so the he could have a cup of tea. The great British solution to all of the world's problems hey a good old cup of tea.

He sat there looking completely bemused and totally at a loss as to how to resolve the situation. Calling the Fire Brigade was suggested and I have to admit I quite liked the idea of getting a firemans lift from our little emergency although I doubt I could have handled being shame faced in front of the other residents. This was very embarrassing!

I went back to my bed and wanted no further part of it. It was 2 am in the morning for Christ's sake. Everyone retired for the night including Dad and it was decided nothing could be done to resolve the situation until the morning.

It was now Sunday morning and that was my favourite day for a lie in but that would not be possible as members of the local council had now shown up and were shouting instructions through the letter box to stand well clear.

God knows what it appeared like to the other residents listening on the landing. It must have sounded like a sort of hostage situation as very large holes were being drilled into the access door to the flat.

There are 26 flats in the fucking block and ours is the only one that could bring this scenario to the table. Lunacy at its finest! Life on the front line with "Silly Bollox" always proves to be eventful.

If the cat flap had been introduced it's not like anyone would have got out any quicker but at least I could still have nipped in and out to complete my toilet duties as they were needed.

The deadlock could not be repaired and was thrown in the bin as scrap and we now live with a big hole in the door where the lock once sat. I bet the police would not be able to believe their luck if they ever needed to pay us a visit again.

It seemed more and more that my little retreat was the safest room in the house and I would prefer being in there more often than not. I would only come out to watch a little TV now and again and I considered even getting myself a small portable in my room and I would have all I needed. Well maybe a sunbed as well. I was definitely staying in here for the remainder of the morning and pushed the door closed because I didn't fancy being in the vicinity when he gave the three teenagers the almighty roasting. I was sure they were about to receive.

He wrote to Charlie Bronson telling him that if he thought that he had it hard in solitary in the cage at Wakefield prison her should try being confined for 24 hours or more with three troublesome teenagers and an annoying little bitch. He couldn't mean me surely!!

When the girls finally left they did so in a very sheepish manner and have yet to pay a visit since which I thought was quite rude and was sure to put him in a bad mood so I decided to make an extra effort to help him with the day's chores. Once I noticed the washing machine cycle was complete I dragged the basket over and pulled the clothes out with my teeth and deposited them in the basket. Today would definitely need to be about a little team work as I did not wish to upset him further.

I was treading on egg shells but could understand his anger. Teenage girls hey! Who would have them? Whoa! Wait a minute though I would be thirteen on my next birthday; I couldn't see me causing a fraction of the problems though. I was a good girl L.O.L. Maybe not all of the time I suppose but I was certainly better behaved than the ones who had just departed. No way would you catch me letting myself out to meet boys in the early hours. Well ok! Maybe I'd be tempted if there actually was a cat flap and I could sneak in and out!!

Ten out of ten for effort girls but you got caught and can see you are going to be spending a good period on the naughty step. They took the easy step and simply stopped coming around to visit and if I was honest I preferred it because it was much more peaceful for us both.

Originally I used to think it would be nice for me to have other females in the flat until I realised I would always be the one left out because they would always close the bedroom door in my face and I had to sit on the landing and listen to all of the girly giggling and loud music from the other side of the door.

But now they were no longer in attendance I decided to explore a little and have a little look at what I had been missing out on. I would need to place the laundry basket up against the bedroom door to reach the handle but I would very quickly gain access. OMG! I wouldn't dare keep my own room this untidy! Empty bottles and cans of pop were strewn everywhere and Dad couldn't have been in this room and seen this or he would have gone ballistic. I tiptoed through the debris and made my way to the corner that had mainly caught my eye the moment I had entered the room and quickly jumped up onto the revolving chair. Of course I had a few spins on it for a little fun but stopped in next to no time to focus on why I had chosen this spot and there in front of my very eyes was the biggest array of girly accessories I had ever laid my eyes on.

I was in the make-up department! I tried on numerous lip sticks and false eyelashes and set about making myself look even prettier than I already was. This was luxury to a girl such as myself and I practically lived in this room for the next week or so practising my procedures over and over until I had mastered all of the techniques. Not that Dad ever noticed because by now he was going through one of his roaming about periods, naked, and mumbling to himself. I would test that he was "in the zone" by singing

Green Door by Shaking Stevens but would get no reaction whatsoever. He would certainly be on a different planet for the foreseeable future I thought to myself but I cared little because I was busy practising how to be a perfect little lady.

I would also set about cleaning the room up a little whilst I was in there and that was a task in itself when I tell you two bin liners would be filled to the very top. Sometimes Dad would shout me when I was only half prepared and we would need to set off like that with my make-up incomplete. We would get many stares as we walked through the town but when would you people begin to understand that we simply had a very strange relationship.

I must have looked like something out the film "A CLOCKWORK ORANGE" while I flaunted about with mascara over just one eye. On the plus side I would be much better than the girls and the make-up had found its way to my face and not all over the bedroom floor. The longer the girls stayed away the better as far as I was concerned because I was certainly having a lot of fun.

No one even seemed to want to apologise for what had happened and so I could see this situation lasting for quite a good while yet. I needed peace and quiet throughout the flat right now anyway now I had taken the decision to write my memoirs but as and when I needed a little release and a bit of time out I could make for the make-up room and get the rouge and foundation out. Not that I needed much foundation as my complexion was quite smooth.

We soon got back to a little normality and Dad just preferred not to discuss the door issue. He did seem a little jinxed in that area though because he either had the police kicking the door in or failing that his "guests" damaging the thing. Such is life! Or should I say such is Dad's life!

CHAPTER 16

More bad news arrived from the DWP and it seemed the finances weren't going to improve any time soon. The poverty trap was now in full swing and biting our ankles at every turn but we had survived before and would do so again. I had begun to get a little arthritis in my back legs and I supposed I would be the next one to be sanctioned by the fucking medical review board. They never seemed to leave us alone and the mail delivered to our address seemed to just consist of official brown envelopes.

Dad had good friends and they had donated food here and there and especially in the pet department and it would be no exaggeration to say that I had enough dry and also tinned dog food to last for the whole of the next year. People in the town would always show a lot of consideration to me and I would always feel that I was a very special little dog that was very much loved by everyone concerned.

He hadn't even been in a public house for three months and had minimised his smoking. What more did they wish him to do? We were already completely on the breadline.

We definitely needed a change of scenery and when we were invited to accompany friends on a caravan holiday to Yarmouth we jumped at the chance. I couldn't wait to pack and because the weather was nice at the time I chose to travel quite lightly with just a few pairs of shorts and flip flops. On occasions such as this no-one would enjoy the coast more than me as I would spend every waking minute in and out of the sea. Water and I just seemed to be a match made in heaven and I would always be dripping wet and be the cause of lots of children's laughter as they gathered round me. I could swim like a beaver for hours at a time and would love entertaining the children with my exploits in the water. The caravan was very comfortable and I enjoyed seeing my Dad in a relaxed mood for a change sleeping in until late morning. No brown envelopes would be getting delivered to this address for sure and so he could finally sleep soundly.

I on the other hand, would be up at the crack of dawn each day and had soon got my bearings although it was quite easy considering big arrowed signs indicating BEACH could be found at practically every corner of the camp site. I would prepare a few corned beef and tomato sandwiches along with crisps and other snacks and place them into my little Tupperware box and wrap everything into my Scooby Doo bath towel and head towards finding myself a prime spot on the beach. Dad would always know where to find me when he woke up because I was completely obsessed with water. He had only given me one rule and that was that I mustn't go in the water on my surf board unless he was there at the time with me. I appreciated his concern but he should have also taken time out to observe me doing handstands on the board whilst I was surfing to show him how I had mastered the waves but he was always fearful that I would be swept out to sea and so I bided by his rules and never surfed while I was on the beach by myself. I would sunbathe and enjoy my picnic until he had got out of bed and joined me at a later stage. The only drawback to the holiday was I would not be allowed in the social club that was on the site but I would be very contented in the caravan by myself and in actual fact it gave me an opportunity to catch up on all of the soaps on the TV and just unwind after I had been swimming all day.

This was the life and I wished more than anything that we had the money to stay here for the remainder of our days. For that week we never had a care in the world and it was plain to see the change in my Dad's demeanour. He was much more visibly at ease within himself and many of his complex personalities were nowhere to be seen during our stay.

I was an easy dog to please and would never need any of the overpriced toys from the shop by the beach. If I was given an empty pop bottle I could chew and amuse myself with that for hours and I would never be satisfied until I had finally separated the screw top from the neck of the bottle. I would chew any bottle to within an inch of its life and leave little segments of plastic scattered everywhere. It would be a noisy practise but if it kept me quietly amused then Dad would throw me one at every opportunity. Again it would amuse the children because I could always be seen carrying a bottle in my mouth for mile after mile.

Dad never forgot any of his friends who were in prisons! The first thing he would do on any holiday at all, would be to grab a handful of postcards and send them to different prisons throughout the country ensuring his friends wouldn't be forgotten. He would call them "hostages" and his policy in life was never to leave any wounded behind. He was a very considerate man that way because he had spent many years in prisons and understood the importance of contact from the outside world. I was certainly thankful that I had him in my life. Here was a man who put everyones needs before his own. I was proud to have been accepted as part of his team.

Our stay in Yarmouth was very much needed, although I never seen much of the actual area itself, preferring to spend the majority of my stay on the beach by the sea. Some of the customary gulls I had come across whilst there turned out to be related to the ones I had met when I had visited Dawlish Beach. Distant cousins so to speak, coast to coast and I also got on with them very well.

I was certainly getting some mileage on the clock and I would never be one of these poor unfortunate pets that got left in boarding kennels and left to wonder what was occurring. Where Dad went then so did I, or so I thought!!! Until a trip to Torremolinos came up on his agenda, but not on mine, as I will explain in a later chapter. But for now this was a very pleasant break.

Everyone knew my name within days of our arrival and all of the children would run to me excitedly and I had no shortage of volunteers prepared to accompany me on walks around the camp. My height, or lack of it, always seemed to add to my cuteness and all of the small children would make a fuss of me and run towards me. I liked being popular because I could always see how people greeted my Dad warmly and I so wanted to be exactly like him and grow up in the same mould. We had no enemies from what I could see at all, unless you took into account police, council officials or the odd door security that is L.O.L.

There cannot be a happier picture than one of a dog bounding through sand or water. I have put photos of my holiday within the book for all of you to see just how happy I was. I was a little bit pissed off that I wasn't allowed in the club but I still didn't let it spoil my holiday. I was to hit my teens because I am thirteen on my next birthday and I couldn't understand why I wasn't permitted in there! Jesus! Did they think I was going to have a dump on the dance floor or something? I would have just had a couple of gin and tonics and staggered home just the same as the others.

It was brilliant weather and everything about this holiday was much needed unless of course the DWP had secreted some of its staff in one of the few beach huts that were scattered about. All of the recent Benefits Britain Programmes highlighting the supposed scroungers amongst us, perhaps we would be looked on in a bad light for having a holiday. None of us would be permitted in the eyes of these judgmental people.

While we were in the local café the headline of the national paper had caught my attention and apparently the Co-op had sustained record losses of 162 million in the first part of the financial year. Well I fucking hoped they weren't going to be pointing the finger in our direction because we had been barred for the past six months. I had only ever taken the one block of cheese away and although "Silly Bollox" liked his coffee I doubt very much he had taken anywhere near the amount of the losses.

It went a long way towards explaining that many more people were in the very same boat as us. Poverty was more widespread than many people would care to admit. Once the holiday was over we would soon get the chance to see which further austerity measures had been put in place. Times seemed to get harder and harder for the likes of us but there still seemed to be a never ending supply of lobster to be eaten and champagne to be quaffed by the very same people implementing all of the austerity measures.

I was going to get a few sticks of rock to take back as presents but sadly we had ran out of money. This is the reality of living on benefits, the need to eke out every last penny before the government take that last one from your grasp. We were poor but happy and I would always prefer having the same standards, morals and principles as my Dad. He didn't let money rule his world and I intended to be the same.

We enjoyed the holiday so much that we placed a deposit and rebooked for the following year but due to our poor finances we would lose the booking and the deposit because we hadn't kept up with the payments. It upset me a little because I was really looking forward to a return visit. It was and still is at the top of my list for favourite holiday spots visited. So it is with a heavy heart we packed our cases to head off back to the Midlands where no doubt numerous dilemmas awaited us upon arrival. It was reaching the stage where even I felt the need to have my own personal psychiatrist and to have a lay down on a settee and discuss my issues.

At least we had made the most of the last day and remained as long as possible. This would also have the added bonus of arriving home late evening and making straight for our bed, whatever problems waited could be dealt with the following day. We both tramped over the mountain of mail at the back of the door because it would be very unwise to peruse the contents right now.

I checked myself out in my full length mirror and discovered I had become quite bronze, tanned and certainly looked very lean and athletic. I would definitely consider once again the purchase of a sun bed for my room to keep my tan topped up. I was burnt a little here and there but I presumed that to be my ginger genes.

I still wasn't tired so to kill a little time I made a list of other items I wished I could have in my room. A bookshelf would be among the main requirements in case I also became a best-selling author, like Dad, and needed to write more at a later stage. I eventually fell asleep in a happy frame of mind.

CHAPTER 17

It was my birthday shortly after we arrived back and by now I had already been given much more independence so it came as no surprise that I was actually given clearance to go to town alone. What he didn't know was I had already been doing that for the few months previously and even the bus drivers were familiar with me and the routes I wished to take. I knew all the stops and that I could travel at 15 minute intervals. When I first did it I had chosen a bus stop with other waiting passengers and just hopped on at the ankles of one of them giving the impression that I was accompanied. It was only a matter of time though before I readily sat at one of the stops alone and the driver would pull over and whistle me on board.

But on this day I set off with my bump bag wrapped around me containing my birthday money. I wasn't really intending to buy anything, I was intending to treat my two canine friends who were homeless and would sit with the local busker, who was their owner. I so wished I could take them home but the problem was Dad would hit the roof if the busker was also in tow with the customary can of special brew. Stray dogs were one thing but stray alcoholics' a completely different kettle of fish.

I dismounted in the bus station and made my way around to the shop door area that I knew my friends would be sat in, with a few treats, I had brought along with me. Their Dad didn't seem as drunk as what he usually was, so perhaps not a lot of money had been thrown into his hat today. Well no way was he having any of mine and that's for sure. I felt sorry for my friends and that was the only place my sympathy laid.

Dad had been quite a heavy drinker but he had stopped now and he had stopped doing street drugs which had to be beneficial for him. He had gotten himself in a lot of trouble selling drugs, but I had to admit that period of his life seemed exciting. I wished I had been about at the time and I bet he did too, now he could see how I was capable of travelling incognito.

When a St Bernard dog tramps through snow blizzards, with a barrel of brandy around his neck, to warm up anyone who was stranded in snowdrifts. I could have been the exact same if someone had got stranded in a living room with no drugs. I could have been the rescue dog that made all the difference. A professional courier service that operated around the clock, I could have used public transport during the day or scampered along the towpath on an evening. It all seemed rather glamourous although having said that I wouldn't have fancied the three years imprisonment, my Dad got, very much. I'd rather have got my sunbed and bookshelf a bit quicker though with profits involved. L.O.L.

Dad and many of his old circle of friends had long since retired from criminal activity, but all of these new government measures had driven many of them back down their old routes and I feared he would do the same. He had already begun to shoplift, which he shouldn't really need to be resorting to at the age he was. It was a means of survival I suppose because his back was to the wall. He would joke that most prisoners used to be allowed to have a budgie in a cage in their cells, "don't worry Stella because dogs might be allowed in the cell now" he would say. Oh I wasn't worried! Well the only thing that worried me was you were such a stupid arsehole that you'd even think I'd want to be in a cell with you! Voluntarily!! Excuse me mister but I think you need to start doubling your medication you crazy twat!

He had been lucky only getting three years because some of his friends had been given ten years each for importation of five million pounds worth of cannabis. Ten years!! Ouch! Trust me Stella Ginnelly wasn't even going behind a cell door for TEN MINUTES.

Things had to take a turn for the better soon because many belts had been made to tighten up, including my own! When Dad ever went out the fire and the television would both be left on with me in mind, but that was not the case no more, as both would be switched off now more often than not.

When he was out now I would read the books he had written so I could learn even more about him. Upon reading I quickly came to the conclusion there was no hope for him. He had always been mental throughout his life and I'm afraid he would remain so for whatever period of time he had left. When I retired each night I would always make sure I lit a candle for him and said a small prayer. Let's be realistic though it would take a sight more than a candle to gain salvation for this crazy individual.

I, on the other hand, had only recently been corrupted and could easily be saved from a life of crime. The problem was though that I liked living life on the edge of things. My formative years had been reasonably quiet and peaceful, but now I would see more adventure in a single week than I would have done the previous year. I decided I was happy to be exactly where I was at the moment in time, being a gangster's moll or whatever the term was for us girls.

I'd read through most of his books and I intended mine to be just as gripping. His life had been quite sad until a tutor in a prison told him he had a masterful style of writing and I don't think he had ever put a pen down since. He helps everyone with any paperwork or letters to authoritative bodies that they feel incapable of doing. He has even recently written to the Pope at the Vatican on behalf of someone, I kid you not! He had to google the tern to use and apparently ifs YOUR EMINENCE. Yes he definitely spends his whole life with a pen is his hand doing one task or another.The friend who he had helped recently by way of gratitude suggested he would take him to Torremolinos in Spain. Now we are talking I thought! The only way is up especially if that's up in a plane. His friend Rafael was half Spanish and knew people who lived out there. Tracey and her two daughters and his daughter Kayleigh was on the guest list. Oh yes! Lots and lots of girls! This holiday was sounding to be the one more and more by the minute. Kayleigh's black Labrador, Daisy, was my best friend although we looked a very odd couple when in each other's company .Ebony and ivory. Little and large, black and white, the pair of us completely different in all aspects. Daisy didn't seem too excited about it all but I just put it down to her being fatigued and so didn't press her on the matter. In contrast I could not contain myself and after a restless night's sleep; I was in town early to the Pound shop to purchase castanets and a Spanish phrase book. I was also after a sombrero but couldn't find one nowhere! Ole! Ole! I would click my paws together constantly, click my castanets and anyone who spoke to me on the bus I would say "Garcia's"! On seeing Dad's face when he spotted my presents I knew instantly that I had yet again read the situation completely wrong and I wouldn't be passing through flight control anytime soon. You bastard! You bastard! I was incensed.

All of them drugs you had managed to smuggle into the country and yet you couldn't smuggle a tiny thing such as me in the other direction. You bastard! All of the "Oles" from me had come to a halt and the castanets had clicked for the last time. It was a heavy blow to take and I wasn't the best dog to be around for the remainder of the week.

To top it all off I was now discovering that I was going to be stopping with a girl called Claire and I recoiled in horror because I knew full well which pet she had at her house. The ever so frisky Bud! Who remembers him then? He would try and mount me at every opportunity for the next seven days and I had what I can only describe loosely as a nightmare stay for the next week. Bud would end up with several scars in and around his mouth where I had rejected his advances. Jesus! I only had to look in his direction and he would be up and running about with a semi on. Give it a rest Bud! Go on get in your basket and rock yourself to sleep.

I hated my stay; I didn't dare turn my back on this predator because he would mount my back in the blink of an eye. I wasn't having the best of times and I hoped and prayed that Dad's holiday was proving to be just as disastrous. Now I had heard him telling everyone who wanted to listen, how he was going to use the holiday to detox himself and have a little bit of rehab. Yawn! Yawn! I had heard it many times before. I would be correct yet again!

He had no sooner left Malaga and arrived at his destination to stay with Tracey and her daughters when he bumped into two random strangers with tattoos on their faces. This shit can only happen to him. They turned out to be Russian Mafia who seem to be everywhere in Europe nowadays. After a little light hearted banter with the main topic of conversation centring around Russian Prisons and English Prisons one of the Russians ran his index finger along one of his nostrils and calmly asked "Do you like this English?" That seemed to be the tag name that was from hereon going to be used to refer to Dad. English!

If Ivan the terrible had known Dad even a little he would have known that "English" certainly does "like" but he is meant to be detoxing. So within an hour of departing from the plane and into his detox he now found himself in some strange Moroccans high rise flat with the Russians.

Rehab went well then hey!! You couldn't make the fucker up!! That must have been the longest week of my whole life and as much as I was angry with him. I knew once I seen him again my tail would whirl at a quicker pace than the police helicopter.

Meanwhile I had more pressing matters to deal with as the predator tried to climb on me yet again. I don't think he had had any sex since the time with me many years before, I suppose he couldn't believe his luck when he realised I was to be staying under the same roof as him for a whole week. Try as he may he would not be getting a result from me. To coin a phrase from the famous politician, Margaret Thatcher, the lady is not for turning! Or better still to coin one of the Spanish phrases I had learned. ADIOS AMIGO! VAMOOSE!

CHAPTER 18

Dad said he would never go to Spain again after all of the escapades in Tenerife. I fully expected him to arrive home early yet again because he was like a fish out of water in foreign countries I had an image of him coming off the plane in a sheepskin coat like Phil Collins in Buster. He and foreign countries didn't seem compatible at all.

He was a typical no nonsense Yorkshireman and if I could have chosen my own place of birth it would have been the same area. He wasted no time in coming to collect me from Claire's. As they sat chatting about the holiday she informed him that me and Bud had got on really well and even suggested the odd sleep over for us at both homes. No way on this earth! I thought unless I had cast iron pants or a chastity belt on. Sleep overs my arse! I would be happy to never lay eyes on Bud again the rest of my life.

But it sounded like Dad had a good holiday and was full of laughter and funny accounts of events during his break. I listened to the stories albeit very enviously. By now though I had accepted the situation regarding the transportation of dogs on air flights and appreciated how difficult it was for me to accompany him.

Not to worry though! He was home now safe and looking and sounding very fresh and recharged. While he was in this energetic and elated mood he took what he thought to be the positive mood to decorate the living room. This is where the lunacy comes into play again because I knew where this would lead. I had been here before!! Not pleasant experience! Trust me! The last time he had chosen to do it, for the next few weeks after completion I would be walking round like I was suffering from some sort of mould, my fur was splashed with that much green paint. Not by choice I might add. Dad just never fully understood that things should be covered up. I doubt he had ever heard of the existence of ground sheets or dust covers. From the very moment he flipped the lid from the paint tin, from thereon no item of furniture or fittings were safe, including me!!

This occasion was to be no different, I would make a conscious effort to remain in my room and only venture out when it felt safe to do so, which wasn't very often. When I came out one time to check on the progress I could not believe my eyes. As I watched him frenziedly applying the paint, he would keep returning to the wall he had done previously to check and wonder why it was taking so long to "dry". Yes, it appeared to have many "damp" patches but I could see already he had made a major error. I couldn't help but laugh because I had just read the labels on the tin and discovered one was Matt and the other one was Silk! So we now had a combination of two different paints on the wall and he couldn't understand why? Even for the next week or more he would return to the same walls to inspect and try to understand what he had done wrong during the process.

I could tell him in an instant what he had done wrong. His mistake had been that he probably hadn't taken his medication the dozy twat! Even to this day he has not got around to correcting his mistake and we are living with walls that are half shiny and half dull. I imagine that's exactly how it would look on the inside of his head because he certainly never engaged his brain to its full capacity.

On the plus side my pure white fur had managed to retain its colour because wisely I had chosen to stay well away from the "manic one" and his brush strokes. Not much else had escaped his attention though, as I noticed the television, the coffee table and all of the furniture had not escaped his attention.

He would stand, with his hands on his hips, proud as punch at what he had managed to complete. It was at these times, I wished I could have all his psychiatric team in attendance, let's all sit down and have a proper team meeting because this man was seriously "off the wall". In actual fact, each time he decorated it always seemed to be in the sort of light pastel type colours, you would tend to find in psychiatric wards, which he had spent many long periods on.

I thought he should still be on one of the fuckers to be honest. There was one here who had escaped the net and who needed to be safely under lock and key. But you had to love him I suppose! I supposed he had been put out to graze! Very much a case of care in the community, it seemed I had been given the short straw, the task of looking after him and tending to his needs. I would attempt to do it to the best of my capabilities, but my only wish would be that he didn't want to be decorating my own room anytime soon. I would definitely be purchasing a NO ENTRY sign from the Pound Shop sometime soon.

"It looks nice Stella doesn't it?" He asked at these moments, the safest bet is to nod in agreement or failure to do so will lead to him flipping the lid off yet another tin of paint. The reality was that it was the biggest botch job since his last previous botch job, also we now needed new carpets and furniture.

The best bet would be for him to put the kettle on, take his medication and call proceedings to an halt. The diary of Adrian Mole wouldn't have a patch on the diary of Stella Ginnelly aged thirteen and a half . I would witness things that would make any of your toes curl. Had I chosen to keep a diary, it's the sort that would be serialised in Sunday Newspapers, the revelations would be that sensational. How many more mental cases such as this one roamed about freely without very much supervision? It was certainly food for thought!

He was in my care though and I had learnt long ago when he was having an "episode". The signs would be easy to spot; nudity would be the first sign of any concern. On a scale of one to ten I would guess "nude decorating" would be a nine or ten, but when he had taken his clothes off later to have a bath. I noticed that large sections of his body were covered in paint; obviously I must have been asleep and missed that period. I bet the neighbours passing by hadn't though. The blinds would always be wide open, I laughed as I pictured people had been walking by at some stage and looking in would have probably seen him naked as a Jay bird painting away, like it was the most natural thing in the world.

No two days were ever the same in this home, if nothing else the days would be constantly filled with laughter and strange events. I hadn't been around that long, what seemed to shock and surprise me would not have the same effect on the neighbours because they had grown accustomed to his "untoward behaviour" I guessed! It wasn't his fault he was this troubled, he'd had a very trouble start in life and had carried the aftermath with him throughout. Even sleep never seemed to come to him easily, I would often hear him shouting and talking to himself in his sleep. At these times I could often be found going up the stairs in my nightie, my hat with a little bell on and also a lit candle in a saucer, to check on his well-being. The sound of the little tinkle from my bell would soon seem to placate him in some way letting him know that he wasn't alone. I would blow out the candle and curl up by his feet for the rest of the night. After all we were a team and I most certainly felt responsible for him.

I would need to take the rough with the smooth and the good would far outweigh the bad days so it was certainly worth it. I would need to keep his behaviour under wraps though, because if any of his medical team knew how his behaviour was deteriorating, then the men in the white coats would be showing up sometime soon. And it wouldn't be the decorators!!

He had recently found out that the man who had typed out his recent best seller for him, had known he was terminally ill, at the time he was doing all of the final editing and chosen not to tell no-one. This was the most fantastic gesture anyone had ever done for him and it affected him badly for a while. When he brought the final draft to Dad and also brought him a few cans and a packet of tobacco, Dad would be eternally grateful. But when he found out that Andy knew he was dying while he completed the work, Dad realised that the gifts that Andy had also brought were a sort of farewell gift to him and admired Andy's strength of character and had nothing but praise for how he had dealt with the situation.

It never helped Dad's moods with all of the recent deaths and funerals he would be attending, but Andy's was the one that sent him over the edge for a while. He was thankful the book NEVER A DULL MOMENT became a best seller when it did because he felt that went a long way towards maintaining the memory of the man R.I.P. ANDY.

I would keep myself low key at these times and would just wait for him to come around in his own time. I would find things to amuse myself and would do nothing to antagonise the situation and just generally keep from under Dad's feet. I wouldn't even badger him for my daily walks and exercise. Should I need the toilet it would be just as easily for me to do my number two on the kitchen floor outside my room because I had long since mastered how to use the dustpan and brush so would clean up after myself. Maybe it would also be a good idea for me to wipe my bum on the brown envelopes that had amassed suddenly, because reading them wouldn't pick his mood up neither, I thought.

Normality, if you could call it that, would soon resume and we could be sighted bouncing about the estate and my tail wag was once again spinning around and from side to side. This was how it needed to be because many people throughout the estate relied on him, to help with problems that had surfaced and more people would contact him then they would the local police it seemed. He would usually resolve matters quicker than them, that's for sure; I was part of the team and felt very much involved.

I had watched police dogs on the TV and felt I could do that quite easily follow a trail given the chance. When people would call and ask Dad could he try to get stolen items back I would curse the fact that they hadn't brought anything that could be placed under my nose and let loose on my own with my nose pinned to the ground lower than Dad's friends when they were sniffing from "the shelf"! I had visions of me racing along at a furious pace with perhaps ten of the local neighbours in tow with knotted nooses and pitchforks at the ready for the culprit once we found him. I was never called upon though, seems a shame hey?

CHAPTER 19

I suppose I'd considered every career available and finally settled on being an author. It had quite a nice ring to it. I would need to find something because I was getting more and more pissed off with some of Dad's friends describing me as a "working girl" and requesting permission to take me out "on the game". I was innocent and quite naive really and didn't realise that "the game" was in fact poultry. I suppose the giveaway should have been them dressed like Crocodile Dundee and all the accessories hanging from their pockets. Bear Grylis they were not! I doubt they'd skinned anything in their whole lives. You could bet I would be fucking skinning them if they called me a working girl one more time.

Dad received a text from Ken Loach informing him that he had made history by being given the Palme d,or award He was only the second man in history to do so at the Cannes Film Festival.

Dad was such a good friend of Ken's that I thought he should talk to him and try to cut a few corners and introduce us to any TV producers he may know with the possibility of me and Dad getting our own prime time TV show on a Saturday night. We were a double act that always had people in fits of laughter and we could be the new Ant and Dec of the TV world. Or failing that Dad could maybe star in D.I.Y. Disaster because that's exactly what it would be.

Wishful thinking, but if we ever reached the screen test stage, I assume it was my task to make sure he showed up fully clothed or God knows what the make-up department would think. I seemed to recall a film from many years ago called THE NAKED CIVIL SERVANT! But trust me it wouldn't have a patch on THE NAKED DECORATOR.

I wanted my booked to be a huge success because I wanted my puppies to be proud of me and I knew in my heart I could match anything that Dad had done previously. We were both artists and quite a clever little duo and it would only be a matter of time before we got invited on to University Challenge or Mastermind.

Dad had already had quite a few cameras in his face and I wanted a little taste of that myself. Yes, I very much liked the idea of me being in demand on the chat show circuit. Jonathon Ross or Graham Norton would have their eyes opened with stories of my early life.

I was already fast becoming the most famous dog of my time and I would need my own Agent anytime soon. I hoped it wouldn't create any petty jealousy with me and Dad although I doubted it would. We had always proclaimed we were a team and that's exactly how it would remain until our final days. This would be just the break we had been waiting for in Ken could put us in touch with the right people.

The only cameras I would have been on prior to that would have been the odd little glimpse of me on the CCTV in the local shop. I say odd little "glimpse" because it would be very difficult to pick me up on the cameras as I was that small. I certainly hadn't been noticed on the few occasions I had pushed a big box or tins of Carling lager with my head. Even some of the customers could not see me at the back of the box and would run from the shop, screaming, believing it to be haunted with different merchandise seeming to move around of its own accord.

I'd had enough of that way of life now and want to put my criminal past behind me. I had been fortunate so far and not even once had handcuffs placed on me. I thought it would be quite funny though, should I ever end up in a court room dock and being asked just how I pleaded and everyone in the room not being able to see me in the dock. All wondering who was the magistrate actually talking to and I would be stood there with a little suit on with arrows and my prison number emblazoned on my chest.

Yes, I had managed to escape all of that which is fortunate, in a way, for the Home Office because I would have been among the first up for a rooftop protest or riot. There's no way I would have ever got paroled because I would have played up at every turn. It would have been best to avoid me and just let me do my weights out on the exercise yard. I can be a moody little dog at the best of times and I would safely say I would have gone crazy being apart from "Silly Bollox" for any great length of time.

I would panic that while I was on remand he would maybe set about painting the whole flat to surprise me when I got out. Ouch! It didn't bear thinking about; he wouldn't last two minutes without me if I was honest. But I suppose it cut both ways and I would feel the same and I also needed him.

But anyway he seemed to be in good mood and that then relays on to me so I went out to play. Typical of any block of flats with a communal bin area, lay the standard bin bags full of refuse but also the usual broken furniture and the obligatory mattress that always seems to be dumped. Not that it upset me as I bounced up and down on it. Higher and higher with the occasional somersault depending on how confident I felt because by now I had noticed, out the corner of my eye, that some of the neighbours were out watching from the landing.

Things were running smoothly until I must have hit one of the loose spots on the springs in the mattress which had possibly been the reason it had been thrown away in the first place. Oops! I thought as I veered off midway through the air at an acute angle and found myself coming down to land on one of the garage roofs. Jesus! That hurt my arse! I could have done with another mattress on the roof to land on, to make the whole routine look like part of the act, but instead I had made myself look a right prat.

The neighbours' laughter could be heard echoing around to add to my embarrassment as they shouted Dad to tell him I was stranded. "FOR FUCKS SAKE STELLA" he shouted from the landing "I'm busy, what are you playing at"? So I quickly decided I didn't want him coming down to rescue me and putting him in a bad mood for the rest of the day.

I ran to the edge of the roof like the Tom Daley of the mattress world, I pretended I had a spring board and took a leap of faith and out in the open and without a thought for my own safety. I did a complete corkscrew on the downward dive and landed in a perfect forward roll on the mattress and rolled from it, stood up perfectly and took a bow. As I saw one or two cigarettes' fall from the mouths of the watching audience.

Oh, I was a girl with many talents and definitely fearless. Although, I will admit I did a few silent farts as I dived from the roof but all's well that ends well. What was all the fuss; I had made it in one piece hadn't I?

I decided enough trampolining for one day though because I didn't want to risk his wrath again. The delayed shock of what I had just done hit home now and my mouth was very dry so I made my way indoors and grabbed a couple of ice pops from the freezer. Enough of being a stunt dog, for one day for me.

I didn't realise until later that one of Dad's sons, Kyle, had a few years previously fallen from the very same garage and an ambulance had been needed at the time and Kyle was unconscious for the next few hours. It had just been one of those accidents that boys do have. Boys will be boys as the saying goes but his ex-partner could not wait to notify her solicitor of the mishap to yet again put Dad in a bad light. Ex's will be ex's I suppose in the same vein, but a little below the belt in my opinion.

He had always been good to me and I was only a dog so I'd no reason to doubt that he wouldn't treat his own children in a kind manner. That would be for them to decide in later years but I hoped they would come to see that their Dad was a good man. I wished that could happen because I would like to meet them. They are my step brothers and sister after all.

CHAPTER 20

I was now on Facebook myself and had a reasonably large following and I considered using my contacts to try and find Dad's children Kyle, Troy and Demi. I knew they lived in Tamworth, I also knew that the last time they had spoken he had been verbally abused. He was so hurt he took the decision to simply back away and leave them alone with their opinions. Obviously it wasn't a very fair outcome but he had already had twenty years of pain from the situation so why add to it any further. If that was their true opinion of him he wouldn't be able to change it. They had said that he didn't exist in their eyes so he accepted that. He was still in touch with his eldest son, David, in Leeds and he had me!

So we just got on with our lives and forgot all about the poison that existed in Tamworth. I don't dwell on that because it upsets my Dad how they spoke to him and he wishes them well but he would have expected his own children he brought up to speak to him a little more civilly than that. Such is life hey!!!

To lighten the mood I had heard that a day out to London was on the cards and some talk of seeing the queen. That talk would need to stop because there was only ONE queen and that was yours truly. Yet another jaunt was in the pipeline then.

Led a very interesting and varied life didn't I, to say the least; I wouldn't swap it for the world. Rail travel, bus travel was all on the house for me and once we finally sorted our free air travel my life would be complete. I had heard so much about EasyJet, I wanted to give it a whirl more than anything and let's be right I wouldn't be complaining about leg room would I?

I was glad I hadn't thrown away my sombrero and I quite fancied a Russian bearskin. I still had lots of adventure in me yet. I was definitely not ready for a blue rinse and a hair net just yet.

I would need to smarten up though, with the London trip in mind, so I looked through my wardrobe to see if I had a nice summer frock and a straw hat to go with it. I hoped we were going for the right reasons with the changing of the guard and trooping of the colours.

It had better not be a drug drop or some other shady business. I know exactly what this idiot usually got up to when he visited this area. If we seemed to be heading towards Brixton or Notting Hill, I would have some serious questions to ask him. I'd rather we were out of that game altogether now that more and more guns were appearing on the scene; and never mind his safety. I had feared for mine once or twice, when I had laid eyes on some serious gangster dogs. Who had looked me up and down with contempt and no way were they tearing my cute little arse another hole.

It had better be a tourist visit and seeing the sights or I wouldn't be very pleased. I had heard plenty of rumours about the size of the fountain in Trafalgar Square and I wanted a little swim in there. Nuneaton Council could shove theirs up their politically correct arse.

When we arrived in Euston I was open mouth at how busy it was; I wondered if Dad looked back on this place with fond memories or not considering this is where he slept rough when he had just hit his teens. I couldn't have imagined it to have been a very pleasant experience at all. He took it all in his stride and was very familiar with his surroundings. I wished I had been with him back then because I figured it would have been very lonely for him.

A small child began to cry when he dropped his ice cream and his mother was at a loss as to what to do. Have no fear Madam! Step aside for a moment. I would lose no time whatsoever in shoving my face into the spillage and readily disposed of the milky mess and licked my lips in satisfaction. Dad had already told me his friend who had paid for the trip was quite stingy and not to expect any treats and so the ice cream was a bonus.

We whiled away an hour or two in the West End just browsing around the shops and viewing some of the sights. The decision was taken to go down the Mall and have a look at the

Queens residence, Buckingham Palace, which I had heard so much about. Arrangements were made that should any of us get spilt up and lost we were to meet back at the fountain in Trafalgar Square. Good call as it happened because it was about to become a very eventful day indeed.

We mingled in with all the other visiting tourists. Many of them were of an oriental appearance and seemed to spend every waking minute clicking away on their very expensive cameras. I attracted quite a bit of attention due to my size and many snapshots were taken while I kept changing position and striking different poses. They laughed like hyenas and pointed and chatted away in Cantonese or whatever tongue while they found it amusing that Dad was talking to a dog. If only they knew the actual truth because Dad was actually talking to himself. I know the signs!! He was having one of his episodes and I hoped and prayed it would soon pass over.

As we gathered by the gates to the palace, I pushed my way further to the front by slipping through the other tourists' legs and found myself pressed right up against the gates with a clear view. I was hoping to come across the world renowned Corgi dogs I had heard so much about, because I felt we had a lot in common. They also were "ginger nuts" and it would be nice to compare lifestyles.

Through the gate I observed a few small tennis balls on the lawns within the grounds and without thinking I was under the barrier and racing towards some of my favourite playthings. I could always be found tearing and ripping these balls to bits and today would be no different. I was gnawing away like a little beaver and having fun when I realised lots of men were running towards me in an agitated state and shouting words of warning. I sat up and looked around to see who had dared cause this discourteous intrusion but I could see no-one else in the near vicinity. Taser!!! I heard one of them shout, as some electric current whizzed past my ear, missing me by centimetres. OMFG!! I was the object of their attention. Apparently I had triggered sensor alarms and every available man had been scrambled. Even the Corgis, who I had foolishly thought I could become friends with, had come running and barking.

I would need to sprint quicker than I had ever done before in my entire life. I went under the barrier a sight faster than I had entered it. I ran and ran with my heart pounding, thinking I may end up in the Tower of London. Off with her head!!

I ran through the crowd and could hear all of the cameras clicking away as I was in full flight. I had always wanted to be headline news in the media BUT not for the wrong reasons. I could see it now. **JACK RUSSELL BREACHED SECURITY**. I was completely out of breath by the time I stopped running and concealed myself in a bush until I could gather my thoughts. How would I get out of London now because the capital was on high alert due to the recent terrorist incidents?

When I finally reached Trafalgar Square, I retrieved a straw from an empty McDonald's milk shake cup. Then I waded into the fountain and submerged myself in the water, I used the straw to access air while I remained beneath the surface.

This wouldn't go down well with Dad, if he had heard about it. I would be grounded forever, if he knew anything of today's antics. Why did this shit always happen to me? But I excelled myself this time; I would be in the deepest shit ever once we got home.

I had recently read that her majesty had been allocated in excess of £300 million pound to renovate her property and perhaps we could come to some arrangement for any inconvenience I may have caused. If I managed to get home I promised myself I would write her a very sincere letter of apology and offer Dad's services as a painter and decorator. I would obviously need to forge his references and definitely not send any accompanying photographs of his more recent work.

I spotted Dad and his friend through the water and surfaced gasping for a clear intake of air and instantly realised I was in a lot of trouble due to the recent events. I was to be concealed in Dad's knapsack and by passed security checks at the train station; we quickly made for the platform to board the next available train to the Midlands. Fearful for my safety I remained in the bag for the whole of the journey and hoped we had now escaped the attention of the security services. Just to be on the safe side we decided to change my appearance and purchased all of the necessary requirements to dispose of my "ginger nut". For a little dog I got myself into a few scrapes didn't I? I thought as I placed my head over the kitchen sink, the solution had been prepared and I was about to become a strawberry blonde as the rubber hat was placed on my head. Or maybe I could get away with just a few highlights!!!

I hoped I didn't have to change my name because I loved my name Stella and so did everyone who I came into contact with. I was more than relieved to be home but somehow or other I was sure my life had many more adventures yet as you will discover in later chapters!! I looked in the mirror and my transformation was complete and I looked a very pretty little picture. My new identity, all hail the Queen!!

CHAPTER 21

We kept our heads down for a while, literally, because I felt a little bit gay with my new bleached nut. I hoped we weren't appearing on Crimewatch anytime soon but if we needed to get away at all I had some very useful contacts.

I had recently joined a Facebook page called GANGSTER CRIMES NOW AND THEN and I could get practically everything I needed on that site! The page is full of what I can only describe as loveable rogues and I'd no reason to doubt that if I needed any false documents then I could acquire them.

Once the dust had settled we began to lead a somewhat "normal" life again if anything could ever be described as even remotely normal around Dad. We heard on the grapevine that the local school had been burgled and the safe had been taken with all of its contents which just so happened to be all of the monies that were for the children's' outings the following year. When crimes like this are committed it's very much of a low life nature and Dad would take great umbrage and be incensed upon hearing. He set about fund raising and within a week had replaced all of the money and perhaps even more on top. He even had a friend send a cheque from Australia for £500. How far did this man's connections go I would think? Very far reaching!

I hoped it would be the exact same outcome if I needed funding for any plastic surgery to change my appearance. All Saints the school that had been burgled, had refused me a place when I was younger, because I was outside of their catchment area. So I never put my heart into getting on the scent of the burglars. I was just as angry as Dad though because many of the children would have missed out had it not been for Dad and his friends getting the money back. A few of the children at the school were special needs children as well so I would like to take this opportunity to "congratulate" you on your choice of target. Very low indeed! Should your names ever be discovered you will be shown the exits from the neighbourhood with a firm boot up your arses? Enjoy your ill-gotten gains! Scum!

But all's well that ends well and the joy on the children's faces with a thumbs up sign for the local newspaper was worth its weight in gold. We were regarded as super heroes throughout the estate and he decided on the tag names SUPER STELLA and DISHY DAVE!!

Uum! The jury was still out on that one I'm afraid, I thought as I pushed the big full length mirror towards him. Get a second opinion if you want but I'm going to have to involve the trade description people if you really do believe you are Dishy!! Obviously he thought he was pretty!

I'd heard him discussing with a friend about PLENTY OF FISH and I convinced myself he was getting another pet. I was bouncing about in a stroppy mood feeling a little jealous and thinking if some fish come in MY home he would take a lot more finding than NEMO ever, did because I would put him in a sack and release him into the canal. I felt such a fool later when I discovered it was a form of "dating" site and found Dishy Dave's description of himself. What a grade A arsehole!! L.O.L. He had gone round and round the mulberry bush, describing himself, in wondrous detail and it definitely wasn't someone that I recognised. I could have saved him all of that time and effort and described him in three simple words. STONE COLD BONKERS!!!

He had already had a few females at the flat but not many had loitered long enough to even have a second glass of wine. I would go to my room and get my stop watch set and simply wait for the assured exit that was forthcoming. On one occasion a girl had left so hastily she had decamped without even remembering to get her coat. He must have stripped off with this one, I sniggered to myself.

I had been with him a good period of time now and nothing he ever did no more would have even given me cause to raise an eyebrow. Everything just seemed normal as far as I was concerned. Because the cupboard in the kitchen had an ill-fitting door that would not close, he ripped it from its hinges and threw it in the general direction of the bin area. Oh dear! I thought as he glanced towards me as if to say "what"??? Nothing really dearest Father!! As long as he didn't think we were playing FETCH because I'd no intention of becoming involved in one of your episodes today.

Once his meds kicked in it would always be the same and he would have regrets. The only regret I had was that it wasn't the door to the fucking treat cupboard that winged its way to the fucking bin area. It was during these moments I wished I still had my smart phone because I could make an absolute fortune sending these clips into the programme YOU,VE BEEN FRAMED.

I'm afraid that he was fooling himself, if he thought that any prospective bride to be was going to be around him for any lengthy period of time. Unless she was on the same medications that is!! Without a doubt the only female company he was ever likely to have from this day forward would be me!

It still didn't stop me getting jealous though, because every time he went out without me I would sniff him upside down and inside out upon his return. I would soon know if he had been within a hundred yards of another dog.

Without realising it I had become quite possessive, I didn't wish to share him with anyone. I know his every move by now!

Well that's if he is wearing his bifocals, because without them he is blind as a bat, maybe that's his excuse for being naked at times, because he can't find his clothes without having his glasses on; although to be honest I think he preferred being in the buff. I'd stopped trying to understand the reason long ago and just accepted this is the way it was to be.

I was never neglected and was happy in my own little world. So I would just leave him in his own little bubble. Never cause ripples because they always lead to waves were my outlook on life and my present setting. Each day around him would be fun filled and unpredictable and I had no cause for complaint.

His first aid drawer would put any back room in pharmacists to shame, if I eve

r had a sneaky look in there he had every colour capsule or tablet you could imagine, a rainbow of medication. He had experimented with every new "happy drug" that had ever been introduced onto the market. All of the wonder drugs such as Prozac, Librium, Valium or Sertraline had not even touched the sides on this lunatic. I don't know why they even bothered trying because it was clear as day to me that he was one of the cases that would always remain incurable. But so what, you had to love him!

He had been in asylums where the patients had to make pretty pictures tying string around tacks, which I daren't even imagine how they expected that to occupy him. When he was an in-patient at the local Avenue Clinic, I would make my way down the canal and calmly wait outside the building. Until I got an opportunity to go through the revolving door at the ankles of some visitors who were unaware I was there and same again to access the ward. I would need to pass lots of other patients and many of them walking about all leaden footed with food down the front of their clothes. Honey monsters I would call these ones and they would laugh insanely as they seen me; obviously believing me to be some sort of hallucination. One Flew Over the Cuckoo's Nest didn't have a patch on this place and apparently it was Dad's THIRD different stay.

If ever they finally accepted the fact he was unique and nothing could be done the quicker they could resolve the bed space for a more in need patient. It gave me an insight into what goes off in these places, I was that small I had gone unnoticed and would hide under tables or beneath beds. I followed along when the whole ward went for a session called occupational therapy, and witnessed one of the funniest moments I am ever likely to come across.

They were all playing Bingo and the winner of any full house received five loose cigarettes. I kid you not!! Most of the patients were that drugged they didn't even know they were in a different room; let alone how to mark off numbers. It would be the longest game in history culminating in a discotheque with all of the patients dancing, or at least that's how it was meant to be.

This is the reality of the mental hospitals we have around us. Dad to this day is still trying to find out what he was being injected with, back in the day when he was only a teenager, but without success. I could understand in a way just why he was as unbalanced as he was. His own G.P. had now read his first book and commented that he would have been very surprised if he hadn't come out the other side a little unhinged. He had certainly had a rough old journey in life but I was now here to make sure all of that changed. A proper little godsend you might say L.O.L.

I probably sensed the importance of seeing the lay out of the clinic, because I presumed the longer I spent around this bleeding lunatic, there was every possibility that I, myself, would at one time feel a need to be booked in as an in-patient. Looking around on my visit though, it was plain to see that others were much more affected by their mental illness, and if anything I was a little blessed in that respect, that Dad was more in control. It's a sad state of affairs to admit that he was one of the saner ones in there. He would never be in there for long though.

I suppose it was a sort of refresher course to remind him of what had made him "nuts" in the first place. He would be treated over a short period, have his batteries recharged, wound up like a clock with a key in the back and then released back into the public domain. It would serve its purpose but only for a short period until the madness returned. Very similar to placing a sticking plaster over the problem rather than swathing a bandage around it; 10,000 volts of electric shock treatment wouldn't be able to sort this lunatic out.

But as always, I would be there on the frontline to deal with any of the madness when it inevitably recurred. It was always worth it because of the many happy events and periods we shared together. I wouldn't have to wait long for one of our adventures of a pleasant nature although I would give the first one a miss.

CHAPTER 22

All the usual suspects had gathered at Dad's flat. Apparently the Stone Roses had finally reformed and were playing dates at Heaton Park in Manchester. Tickets were like gold dust but Alex Spadavecchia, a good friend of Dad's, had managed to acquire some and I would have to listen to all of their excited gibberish whilst they made all of their plans to travel to Manchester. I would be giving this a miss. I had heard enough of "I wanna be adored" to last me a lifetime and wanted no part of it.

Alex, whose nickname was Spud, would be doing the driving and hotels were booked in advance although Dad would NEVER bother with any of that. He and another friend called Granty would always prefer to "rough it" and experience the proper atmosphere as they called it. I was glad I had chosen not to go because they had slept in a multi storey car park in Deansgate and if that's what they called capturing the full experience they could shove it.

Obviously, the off licenses had taken the decision to stay open throughout the night, with all of the captive trade who were stranded in Manchester until the following morning. Dad and Granty had been to many festivals together and were both durable and could sleep on a clothes line if they were called to do so. Fuck that I thought it would have been a hotel or nothing for me. I'm a lady for Christ's sake! Why would I choose to sleep in a car park in Manchester watching them pair of idiots passing yet another bottle of vodka from mouth to mouth?

The drama didn't stop there, it never did with Dad! Spud decided to stay a further night to access the VIP area at the following night's concert. Dad and Granty however, would need to catch a train home that same day, but not before they had spent the day drinking in Manchester and finishing off the contents of their clip bags. If you know then you know!!!

They would board the train with the customary bottle of vodka and make their way back via Stoke and Stafford to the Midlands. Needless to say they showed back up at the flat in a very sorry state; and if I needed my toilet break I would need to do it quickly before they went into one of their drug and alcohol induced comas.

I was glad that Dad had more than enjoyed the occasion though because that would go a long way towards elevating his mood over the coming days. The Roses were one of the few bands he had not managed to see due to him constantly being detained at Her Majesty's Pleasure in their heyday.

Granty and Dad were the ever presents of any festival whatsoever and had covered some miles between them. Although they could never tell you which bands they had seen because they would be in such an addled state. They would do more "chemical attacks" than any modern day warfare. Pills, thrills and bellyaches were exactly what this pair was about.

I became a little excited myself now to discover that during the coming months I would be getting taken to the Isle of Wight festival. My very first bit festival; I couldn't wait! From being a small dog continually cornered on a back yard I had now visited; Devon, Yarmouth, Cornwall, Truro, St Ives, Teignmouth, Middlesbrough, York, Bradford, Leeds and Dewsbury. While many people had not even left their settees, in Nuneaton, during that period, now I was to be sailing from Southampton over to the festival.

I was such a lucky little dog and realised that more and more each day. The time couldn't pass quickly enough for me, as arrangements were made and changed on a daily basis. Nothing ever ran smoothly with this lot but as long as the final outcome was we were on that ferry I didn't give two hoots.

At this point it is worthy to mention Dad's friend Liam, who was to be the driver on this excursion. Liam was one of life's characters, who was of American descent and had come to this country many years before with the intention of settling. Whilst here he had decided to go and visit Amsterdam, albeit only for a long weekend, he enjoyed Amsterdam that much that he remained there for the next ELEVEN YEARS. That's certainly a long weekend by the stretch of anyone's imagination. These were the sort of colourful characters, Dad always seemed to have in his life and it's what made it so much fun. Liam passed away not long after our visit to the Isle of Wight. R.I.P. Liam, you will never be forgotten in our memories.

The time soon arrived for us to be making the journey, and I would have my face pressed tightly up against the window all throughout the journey not wishing to miss a single thing. I had never been so excited, I was about to go on a boat for the very first time. The Solent is ever such a busy route and at times akin to being on a motorway, there are that may boats, ships and ferries criss crossing each other going in both directions.

I had taken my Parka coat with me in case the weather changed but at this moment in time I was laid on a li-lo on the top deck in blazing sunshine and life, it seemed, couldn't get no better. To say the Isle of Wight is as close to our shores, as it is, it's like going to another country once you have crossed the water. It certainly gives a different feel to a festival I supposed. This was by far my biggest adventure to date and I intended savouring every moment. Little did I realise I had work to do first; there would always be a catch in any of Dad's plans.

Now the usual routine at a festival such as Glastonbury or V festival, would be to scale high walls, which I wouldn't have much, fancied doing. But the Isle of Wight involved wrist bands to gain entry, my Dad's circle of friends would always purchase a certain amount of tickets to gain a wristband and they would be shared constantly throughout the weekend. It had always been a time consuming exercise for them on previous visits due to all of the tramping backwards and forwards. But not this time it seemed!!!

The few without wristbands, would wait outside of the venue, while the ones who were in, would set about pitching the tents and making themselves at home. I would now be given the task, of carrying the "spare" wristbands in my mouth or tied to my collar and making my way past the security to the one's that had waited patiently outside. I would breeze past the security without even causing the slightest suspicion; I doubt that I had even been seen I was that small. This would need doing to access the camp area, yet again to actually enter the arena where the stages for the bands to play were. It was to be a long drawn out process but most of Dad's friends were unemployed and looked after each other; no-one got left behind!! They had camaraderie like no other did this circle, whatever scam that was on offer at any festival, you could rest assured these would know it and be at the front of the queue.

I was to be sharing a tent with Dad and Granty but I really didn't care who I was sharing with. I was just really happy to be here; it wasn't all about the festival, because on many occasions we would drive down to the beach and sea front at Sandown, and eat outside the finest sea food restaurants. It really was just like being on another holiday, I thought as I swam in yet another different coastline.

Nuneaton would always be a town that had more than its share of people in attendance and this time would be no different. Apparently, new rules had been put in place and camp fires were no longer permitted. By now perhaps, thirty people from Nuneaton, had all pitched within close proximity to each other, and had their own little village near enough. I knew nearly all of them in attendance and pretty quickly realised that no-one would be getting much sleep. This lot never slept back in their own home town, so there was little chance of expecting them to drink hot chocolate and bed down here.

The first signs of any confrontation came about with a few heated words about the level of noise. These warnings were ignored by Dad and his friends. Once it began to get cold in the early hours of the morning, a decision was taken to get a stone circle fire going, which did not go down too well with the security. I'd like to point out at this stage, that the people who I was with had been attending festivals for many years. They were certainly more than capable of tending to a fire with no fear of it spreading, but all of this information seemed to fall on deaf ears, with regard to the security, insistent that fire must be put out. By now they had been to bring more and more of their security and a stand off developed.

Oh dear, for fucks sake; I felt like singing a few choruses of the Disney song "let it go" but instead chose to inch my way back into my tent, cover my ears and watch developments from a safe distance. I especially thought it a wise thing to do as I noticed a few of Dad's friends pick up logs from the woodpile with the intention of using them for weapons. Dad's friends were very violent people and had the "scouse" security not taken the decision to climb down a little it would have very much turned into a bloodbath. Certainly not one I would have wished to witness on my first visit to a major festival.

I could remember little or nothing of which bands played, because with this lot it would be the same scenario, as every other one they attended. Tents pitched, fires lit, drugs and alcohol out and everyone in such a messed up state that the last thing on their minds would be keeping to any deadlines to watch whoever. I could vaguely remember seeing a man in a white suit and hat singing "Have a Nice Day" which transpired to be Kelly Jones and the Stereophonics. I would certainly be doing that, I'd already had one of my nicest days ever in actual fact; I never wanted it to end.

At the end of the festival, we would end up staying on the island until the middle of the week, giving everyone a chance to leave with all the hustle and bustle of packed ferries. We would leave at our leisure once the ferries were empty. By the smiles on everyones faces, it soon became apparent, that it had been a profitable outing and no shortage of funds meant we could all live the high life for a few more days. I will drink to that, I was happy to stay for however long everyone intended to.

CHAPTER 23

We would need to camp away from the festival site, for the additional days we chose to stay, as it would require a very substantial clear up of the area. The first night we set up camp, we had done it in darkness, only to discover at first light, we had done so right in the middle of an exclusive golf course and absolutely scorched a big section of the putting green on one of the holes. This could only happen to this lot I thought as I rolled hysterically. Everything was packed in a flash and we were gone long before the first rounds of golf for the day would begin.

Having reached the ferry point only to discover we had to wait an hour for the next ferry, I watched as everyone counted out large wads of money from the weekend trade, in the dance tents and camp sites. It seemed that the ones who were brave enough to smuggle, any contraband into the site, would most certainly reap the rewards, because obviously certain prices are increased ensuring a greater profit margin. He who dares Rodders! He who dares!!

I wasn't looking forward to going back home, but had to admit by now everyone was very weather beaten, fatigued and in need of a good shower and definitely a night's sleep, including myself. Liam was so fatigued that he had nodded off at the wheel, and if another friend Mark White hadn't grabbed the wheel we would have most certainly ended up over the looming cliff. My paw worked furiously trying to unwind the car window, although it may have seemed a selfish act, I would have been out of that window in seconds and waved the other passengers goodbye. That was the one and only, close death experience, I had ever had and wouldn't wish to go through it again.

I was glad they decided to have a wash and brush up and coffee break at the next services, because from where I was looking at the moment in time, I would have had more chance of driving the car and getting us home safely. We had survived the cliff incident but neither did I fancy being the meat in the sandwich between two trucks. I felt I was on borrowed time with these arseholes in charge of my safety and well-being. The highs and lows of the festival fools!!

But I would still hope to be going to another soon and knowing my Dad the way I did that would be sooner rather than later. I wouldn't have thought no dog in living memory would ever be embroiled in all of the activities I got up to. I was a one off, I was unique but then again so was Dad!

I was glad that no melee had taken place with the security though, because I knew Dad's long criminal history involved many incidents of violence and last thing I would want was him to be in prison yet again. I knew about many of his violent outbursts, but most had involved brutalising rapists or paedophiles, and I'd no qualms about him meting out what he deemed justice. He had never shown me anything but kindness, so I would have no hesitation in proclaiming this was the man I wished to spend the rest of my days with!! Being around him, would never mean quiet weekends away in the Lake District or anywhere similar. No way, it was always destined to be a white knuckle ride, but I had fastened my seat belt a long while ago and I was prepared to be with him all the way down the line. The runaway train was the ticket I had chosen to be in my hand.

When we finally arrived home, everyone wasted no time in finding a comfortable spot and going to sleep. Unusually, Dad had forgotten to feed me and sleep never came easily to me on an empty stomach. I nuzzled the door open to my food cupboard but there was no dried food or treats and I was unable to open the ring pulls on the tinned food. I had a little mooch about in all of the bags that had been dumped on the living room floor and came across a Tupperware box that at least appeared to have a little roughage within. I set about chewing a few, they had quite an earthy taste, but I thought anything is better than nothing. As I picked the box up to read the label MEXICAN MUSHROOMS!!

I thought nothing of it as I retired to my basket, for what I thought would be the remainder of the evening. However, within half an hour I seemed to not to be able to focus much and the dog ornaments kept appearing to move. OMFG!! What was occurring? Everything became a mass of colour, it became impossible to close my eyes, so I ventured into the living room and just about everything in there was also moving from spot to spot. I attempted to stop things from moving with my paw but I seemed to have acquired an additional paw. In fact everything seemed to be in double or triplicate as everything danced around and I was in a very confused state. I hoped to fuck, that no one expected me to be doing A MEXICAN WAVE anytime soon because I hadn't a clue what I was doing.

Don't get me wrong, because it was a quite enjoyable euphoric state to be in, and had the rest of them been awake, I could quite easily have seen me doing a little high fiving myself and singing a few choruses of "I wanna be adored". I had a feeling of invincibility but also accompanied by many fits of the giggles as I crashed about. It mattered little how much noise I made, because it would be virtually impossible to wake any of this lot up now their heads rested on pillows. I jumped to the top of the chair by the bay window and laughed at all of the passing traffic that had taken on the resemblance of long American Cadillacs. Just about everything was out of all proportion and nothing would come into focus and it was like I was playing the leading role in a cartoon. I could now understand why Mexicans had siestas, and slept though the afternoon if this is what they ate with their salad.

Boom!! I was more far gone than Baloo in the Jungle Book doing his dance. In actual fact I had begun to dance myself, I had the Sombrero on and castanets from my room. I knocked more and more things over, as I became very clumsy, but instead of being concerned, all I seemed to be able to do was laugh hysterically. I looked at the box on the coffee table where I had left it and was tempted to scoop up another pawful but thought better of it.

A sense of normality returned in the very early hours of the morning and without me hearing a thing, one of Dad's friends had woke up in the other room and came downstairs. Although my vision had returned slightly, I was far from functional, so when I was taken outside for toilet duties and I hit the open air it all intensified again.

What I hadn't realised was that some of the neighbours' had been recently having domestics with each other and took thing to extremes. Standard behaviour for this neighbourhood I'm afraid. But one of them must have chosen to throw a tin of Gloss paint over the family car as a final measure to close the argument. I'd failed to notice meanwhile; just how much paint was spread about the car park at the rear of the flats. In my hallucinogenic state, I had just paddled through all of the excess paint that had failed to hit the car. When I re-entered the flat of course, I had noticed the odd foot prints of sorts, but simply believed it to be yet another part of the strange events, that had taken place all throughout the night.

Oh dear! I would soon be brought back down to reality when Dad started screaming obscenities, upon seeing all of the white gloss marks, throughout the flat as I had walked in many a circle during my mushroom "trip". Calm down dear! I thought to myself or is your memory that short as not to remember the SEVERAL occasions you, yourself, have covered the flat in every colour of the rainbow.

I wasn't in the mood for any long drawn out reprimand, by now due to the nights exertions and I about crawled into my basket. But within seconds, I was pulled by the ear and deposited firmly on the kitchen floor. For the next twenty minutes, I had my paw pads scrubbed with a brillo pad that hard that I wouldn't be able to walk freely for the next few days.

Next time any of your girls decide to go on a diet, please beware of any box with MEXICAM MUSHROOMS on the label, because I don't know about losing weight but you will certainly lose your mind. All in all it was a very pleasant experience but not one I would care to repeat. My ornaments in my room finally stopped dancing and returned to their original resting places; and so did I.

My basket was calling and after throwing my Sombrero onto its nail on the wall, I settled down, snuggled up, and slept the remainder of the day away. Adios Amigos! I'm out of here!

When I awoke and came into the living room and spotted Dad on his knees my original reaction was "FFS he has eaten the rest of the mushrooms". But he was still attempting to clean the paint from the carpet, as he looked at me menacingly. We didn't live in a palace, but the one thing I could say is that he did keep on top of the chores and kept a clean house.

He had spent eleven years in a variety of penal establishments and mental institutions so I'd guess he just had a lot of order and discipline instilled in him. I yawned, nonchalantly, and simply jumped up onto the top of the chair again by the window and laughed inwardly about the previous night's events once I recalled them. It would be much better for me to stare out of the window than make eye contact with "Silly Bollox", because he certainly wasn't in the best of moods. All of the cars had returned to their normal size and there wasn't a Cadillac to be seen nowhere. Wow!! What the fuck had happened there? That still remains as one of the weirdest nights I had ever had to survive and as you all well know by now I've certainly had a few testing ones around this arsehole. And more to come no doubt!!

CHAPTER 24

Most of you will have realised by now that my life very rarely runs smooth but I wouldn't have it any other way. I could never have envisaged meeting some of the colourful characters I have. No semblances of order in their lives, all of it complete madness and mayhem. I have watched may different people wake up on Dad's settee not having a single clue where they are, what they have taken or even which day of the week if was.

I would readily see the perplexed faces while they tried to gather their thoughts and the main thing that would bring them back to the real world would be noticing me in the same room. Hey Stella, come here, good girl!! They weren't exactly that pleased to see me. It just so happened they had found the last piece of the jigsaw to remind them whose house they were actually in.

Many of Dad's friends also had dogs and I had met the majority of them and could rest safe in the knowledge I lived with the best of the lot. I would never give it large or have any attitude with them although it would be difficult not to at times. A lot of them were bitches from the canine world and exactly as in human circles when you get a lot of bitches together the outcome could be disastrous.

Oh how I wished I could have invited some of these around for a "girlie" night in. Especially, if I could get the opportunity to put the Mexican Mushrooms on the menu with the prosecco; now that would definitely make for a very interesting night and soon put a few of them in their place. Some of them were very disloyal and could not be trusted and were jealous of mine and Dad's relationship. I wasn't like that in my nature! I had learned my standards and principles from Dad, who was very towards his close circle and even strangers. He could always be found sat writing to anyone at all in prison. He would never leave them without any extras, even though he could ill afford to be sending people things, he always would and leave himself without. Close friends such as Lee Cas and Chod (R.I.P.), names can be found tattooed on his hands. He always lived his life being friendly towards everyone and I intended to be the exact same.

I had met his entire inner circle and I could understand how he remained staunchly loyal to them because all the lot of them were very likeable rogues. He would be very much proud of the fact that he had never even been the cause of any man even spending one night in a police cell, so I doubted he would have been able to live with himself if he had actually got someone a prison sentence. I'd no reason to doubt him because no-one had a bad word to say about him and he is always greeted warmly everywhere we go.

I'm very pound to walk at his ankle and I never leave his side. If he comes out of a pub toilet, I can be readily found sat outside the door. Obviously, he is recognised as being very loyal and I am only being the same to him in return. If I was eighteen I would have had his name tattooed on my chest by now. I didn't want to be any other dog or in any place other than the one I was now. I liked this life and living on the edge, I was never cut out to be one of those that visited theme parks or preferred country walks. Give me the manic lifestyle that went with this lot any day of the week; anyway apart from that I was too fucking small to get on the rides.

The police would have known all about me by now, I imagined my mug shot would have been on a pinup board, down the station, along with Dad and his friends. A pretty sight that must have looked for any of the officers clocking in for duty every morning; I was obviously the prettiest one out of the whole roll call. I had come a long way from being a little unrecognised breed of dog. I was now readily identifiable, throughout the area; I have contributed a lot and made a conscious effort to raise awareness and improve the image of the Jack Russell.

I have just spent the best part of a month writing this book and I am a very dedicated little dog and once I begin a project there's no stopping me. I've not even sniffed another dog's arse in all that period of time. I've been absolutely covered in ink a lot of the time, but I am hoping the effort was worthwhile. Dad still receives Royalties from his two books and I have agreed to share any profits from this one with him.

Things had to take a turn for the better soon, surely, or were we destined to be permanently poor? Life was a constant struggle for us and especially with the cursed bedroom tax, which had taken a complete stranglehold on our lives. We would need to attend an up market soup kitchen each Monday for a three course meal and the lady who ran it, Sonya, would always make sure food was also available for me. We seemed to be always reliant on one charity or another and it affected Dad badly, because he was quite a proud man. If anything, it was long overdue that Dad received any compensation that was his entitlement. We just needed something to give us a break in our situation and to help keep our heads above water without the need to use a begging bowl. It's the main reason I took the decision to sit down and write my memoirs to hopefully raise our financial status. It's hard to be funny all the time when the reality is living on the poverty line on a daily existence.

I would feel guilty many times because as Gods my Judge I go without nothing; I am numero uno! I get everything I want without even a second thought. All that time ago when I heard him utter the words "we are a team". I had my doubts because of my previous experiences, but I really had found the needle in the haystack; a true uncut diamond.

For all of the poverty in our lives we were certainly rich with laughter. This is possibly our last shot at getting a source of income because both of us have certainly left it a little late to be enrolling in any college. I had been encouraged over and over to write this book and will be quite disappointed if it has no success. It wasn't a lot to ask.

We just went to both sit in our reclining chairs each night with cheese and crackers and watch Paul O'Grady. Dad in his The Who dressing gown and me in my Snoop Dog nightie!! I just wanted to live the life of a little dog and Dad just wants to be left alone in his world of lunacy. Dad lives his life more and more by social media; he is becoming more reclusive because of all of his anxiety and depression. It is fortunate he has me because I give him the encouragement to venture outdoors but failing that his social life had become non-existent. He had not visited a public house for three months because of his lack of confidence. I can honestly say that I have never seen him this low and it's my responsibility to raise his spirits.

I've probably been spending too much time on this book and not paying him enough attention! The last thing you ever wanted to do was take your eye off the ball with "Silly Bollox", or the family home could end up completely demolished or worse still.... Somebody else's property; you wouldn't want this one running loose in your home. I laughed for days when I heard he had got given community service work in his younger days. His was a serious offence so he had been given the maximum 240 hours and he would need to do a minimum of 15 hours per week because he already had a full time job.

There would be the occasional gardening job to do but the majority of it involved decorating. After he had been at one old lady's house that hadn't a clue who he was; she had barricaded herself in the bedroom and rang the police. I thought it might have been because he had got up some of his silly antics. It turned out she had let him in originally, but when she later came across him pasting paper in the living room, she had forgotten who he was and thought she had an intruder. It turned out she was more mentally unstable than he was. That would have took some doing believe me!! As it happens it was probably a wise move to get him out of there because she would have screamed the house down when she seen the quality of his decorating.

God I never tired of his stories and I wished I'd been with him from my very first day as a pup. If this book bombs I's probably be tempted to serialise his escapes in the Sunday newspapers. No amount of medication could even begin to hold him down; he was a proper live wire! Light the blue touch paper and stand well back L.O.L. There had been no shortage of shrinks who had attempted to get to the bottom of this Pandora's Box. I'd studied him at great length myself and decided that should any psychiatrist ever actually get to the bottom of this one, they should be put on the Queens Honours list!

I didn't care about what the flat looked like to be honest, the atmosphere within it was special and I couldn't imagine Dad ever wanting to leave. It consisted of 26 flats with very long landings and I imagined it reminded him of prison and that's why he settled into his surroundings so well. Home from home to him! I had become accustomed to it just as easily, I wouldn't have a problem with him placing a card outside my room with my name and number on it. I was his soul mate and his best mate so I would have no objection to also being his cell mate. As long as it would never involve any roof top protests, throwing slates from the building etc. I would leave that shit to him and his mate Bronson. Or perhaps he would need to do it alone because Charlie Bronson had completely changed his ways now and was a very much a man of peace.

We would only need to correct the behaviour of the arsehole living with me and the world will be a far better place. Although, having said that I would have no problem with Dad's strange behaviour as long as it stayed indoors. He would get tasered in no time out there, causing one of his scenes amongst the general public. He may have had several personalities living within his head BUT every one of them knew to put a bowl of dog food out, so I did not have a care in the world. I was happy and content; if I needed food it was available. Should I ever need a vet's attention it would always be dealt with at the earliest opportunity, so as far as I was concerned I was living in the lap of luxury?

I would be walked ten miles a day and get plenty of exercise with my ball and other toys. I was that healthy with all of my outdoor pursuits, that it would be safe to say, I would outlive many other dogs on the estate. Not bad for a dog in the care of an out and out lunatic hey? Having said that, I had never wanted to pack my cases from the moment I met him, we were a match made in heaven.

CHAPTER 25

Dad had started drinking again; he didn't intend to but he found himself attending that many funerals and toasting his departed friends that it soon became a natural progression that he was drinking upwards to seven pints on a session. Prior to that he had just been having a tot of whiskey in his coffee at the end of each day and had settled into middle age respectability. He really was trying to be sensible and self-treat himself. The only reason he was having the whiskey was to try and cut out his consumption of Zopiclone sleeping tablets. I liked the idea that he was attempting to be a little positive, because with the medical profession nowadays, people like Dad would get overlooked for long periods and left out on a limb. If a psychiatrist can only see one of his patients on a three monthly cycle, than what purpose does that really serve? Dad would be waved off from a meeting and be given an appointment for three months down the line. He could be in tip top shape as he left but two weeks along the way he could be having a major crisis and morphing into his alter ego. For that reason he had no further faith in the profession and felt let down.

It had never been this way when he originally sought medical attention in the early 1970's. Everything nowadays had been cut to the bone and nobody could rely on a truly professional service anymore. I would be left to cope with Dad's episodes when he had them but I was sure I had a calming effect on him because we were constantly in each other's company. Both of us had our quirky little acts of behaviour and he had realised by now I was totally obsessed with water and in particular the canal alongside the flats. I had incensed him on many occasions by my refusal to come out and he had finally found a resolution to the problem. He had bought an extendable lead and I would be allowed now to dive in and swim alongside him as he walked along the tow path. This would go on for mile after mile with all of the people on the passing barges smiling and waving at me and Dad while I paddled along with my paws. Many said I should have been born a fish or enquired if I was in training for the Olympics in a joking manner.

We were regular sights along these walkways and could be found here on a daily basis. In actual fact one of my favourite moments ever happened along here on a dark evening whilst we were walking home from the local public house. Dad had already drunk four pints of his customary Carling lager when he had been informed the lager had run out! The Landlady apologised for any inconvenience but foolishly mentioned that she only had Stella lager. He had decided that there couldn't be that much difference and so proceeded to have a further three pints of the stronger lager. He had very much under estimated the strength of the latter. As we walked home along the canal, I could definitely tell his muttered mumblings were a little different to usual but even I hadn't planned for what happened nest.

While he walked along, in the pitch black, texting on his phone rather than keeping an eye on where he was walking, he simply walked into the water as if walking from a pirates plank. Splash, man over overboard!! I fell about laughing as I watched him flounder about in the water until the realisation set in that he couldn't even swim. It was a funny situation that all of a sudden had turned very serious. Don't get me wrong because the canal was quite shallow, but at this time of night the water would have been quite cold, and the weight of the water on his clothes could have took him under in his intoxicated state. I was at a loss as to what to do and just barked and barked to raise attention. He also had the extendable lead in his pocket or I could have perhaps thrown that to him as a lifeline and towed him out with my teeth. I had visions of the hero dog headlines in the paper but by now he had scrambled his way to the embankment. Although he grazed his knee and elbow clambering out he was now safely laid on the path albeit gasping a little. I had watched incidents like this on TV and knew exactly what to do as I jumped on his chest and attempted to pump the water from his lungs. It didn't take him long to stand to his feet and continue the journey as if nothing had even occurred.

He wouldn't be texting again for the foreseeable future because his phone had remained on the bed of the canal. It was fucking Stella that needed pumping from his lungs, rather than the water, if that's the effect it was going to have on him. I got him to his bed and slept at the bottom to ensure he was alright. He awoke early hours and reached for his jeans to have his obligatory cigarette and commented that his jeans were wet and this bemused him. He hadn't a clue he had been in the water the dozy twat! He, thankfully, had never let a drop of the stronger lager pass his lips since.

On reflection it's a comedy gold situation but on the flip side it could have possibly turned out very different. One off his very close shaves! I doubted it would ever happen again, but I made a mental note of putting him down on my Christmas shopping list, for an extendable lead of his own for when I walked him home. I thought it very ironic that it was Stella the cause of his mishap and also the very same Stella, me, that would be responsible for the rescue. Not one of his better moments, but funny all the same. Very!!

Many of the pubs around the town were dog friendly and I would be always welcomed at any of the venues, although I seemed to have caused a few ripples at one of the local working men's club. I had been going in this club without a problem for the previous two years but new members had been voted on the "THE COMMITTEE". I suppose you've all met them at one time or another, the ones full of their own importance!! One time after I had left with Dad a committee meeting had been called to discuss me L.O.L. You couldn't make it up!! The decision was taken, no doubt after a long heated debate, that I was no longer welcome on the premises. Dad was notified through a third party of the decision. Apparently, they were going to send ME a letter to notify me but they didn't know my address. HA HA.

So I now had my first ban although I had done nothing wrong. I suppose it would do my image as a gangster dog no harm but I felt I needed to recount this story because of its humorous content. Want you all to visualise grown men sat around a table discussing me or any other dog come to think of it. How's about you get a fucking life!! But I would take my ban gracefully and wish you all the luck in the world; with Dad in there should he ever have one of his episodes whilst unaccompanied. One of you would soon be contacting me if he started ordering his beers at the bar stark bollock naked. It would never happen really, because Dad would always remain loyal to me, and if I wasn't welcome he would never entertain the place himself.

The only reason we had ever drank in this club anyway, was because it was very conveniently placed next to the DOORWAY charity that we done a lot of fund raising for. I wasn't a bad dog, and perhaps should have been given a little more consideration because of my charity work, but I now felt I had a sort of criminal conviction because of "the Committees" ruling. Could you all raise your glasses and toast the power of these people wield? The importance of being earnest L.O.L.; like Dad and I cared!

We were more than welcome at every other pit stop in the town so we took it in our stride and laughed at the wild and wicked ways of the world. They would have been the very same pompous people, who done their trade from a building adjacent to our charity and contributed little or nothing to the cause. All hail "The Committee", a band of merry men, adios amigos. I cared little because I was welcomed everywhere else in the town, and had become a very well know character and received treat after treat at all of the shops we passed. I would always weigh an additional stone by the time we walked home through the park.

I loved my visits to the town and would stand and stare in admiration at the bronze statue of the famous authoress George Eliot and imagined a bronze statue of me in years to come after I had wrote many more books. Or maybe a better idea would be to have a bronze statue of "The Committee" sat around a table L.O.L.

It was at times such as this I wished Dad still lived up the North, because in the Working Men's Clubs up there poultry would be openly displayed, on all of the tables, freshly caught that morning, and there wouldn't be much of a rule book to be called upon. If there was, I supposed there only would be the need to have muddy wellington boots on your feet to even gain admittance and every single man in the place with a dog at his side. The North is a completely different setting, though I suppose and still holds out for all the principles the clubs were originally formed for. None of this mamby pamby middle class club circuit that seems to exist in this area. Even the female bar staff up the North wear muddy boots; but the ban was in place and I would need to accept it.

In the future I hoped Dad would take the decision to relocate to his place of birth because I knew in my heart I would thrive in that setting. He had squatted many properties in the past and I quite fancied doing a little of that myself, although it would prove difficult now with the changes in the law. It wouldn't matter if we couldn't, because he had just as many friends in Yorkshire as what he did in the Midlands and they would all give us somewhere to live if he was ever brave enough to make the final move.

I could often sense just how much he missed the area. Originally, he only left because all of the pits and steelworks had closed and he had no means of employment. If work had been available up in that area, I am sure he would never have left in the first place. Even his psychiatric care up there had been much better than what he was receiving now. He would not need to discuss matters with me to any great length. If he ever chose to leave this area and return I would go with him in a heartbeat. A long as we remained together I would be happy wherever we lived.

CHAPTER 26

I could always sense when he was a little homesick, there had been a lot of death and tragedy lately in the area and I could see he was pining for a change of scenery. The very latest incident had been the final straw. A three year old boy, from Tamworth, with an aggressive form of cancer had died suddenly. His name was Charlie, Dad had only recently received pieces of art from his friend in prison Charles Bronson Salvador to contribute for a fund raising day for "little Charlie". The news that he had died, devastated Dad and he was reluctant to inform big Charlie what had happened. He retreated into his shell, like a tortoise for a few weeks, only popping his head out occasionally. Wounds healed but this particular one would be a very heavy blow to recover from and his heart went out to the little boy's parents and the art work would be auctioned to assist them in whatever little means possible.

Dad's behaviour became a little bizarre over this period of time until a few funny incidents slowly made the smile return to his face. He would always be poncing, pruning and grooming himself, obviously in the mistaken belief that he would eventually come across some prospective bride. I cringed as I observed him trimming his eyebrows in the big mirror on the living room wall. You first need to realise he is as blind as a bat without his spectacles. I had witnessed him do this very same exercise on several previous occasions. Always with the same outcome!! He would be pressed tightly up against the mirror and set about the task, with WALLPAPER SCISSORS!!! OMG!! It would always have catastrophic results and any slight trim would become a complete mutilation with bald patches in abundance. He would never discover what damage he had actually caused until he replaced his glasses. He would pretend to himself that he had done a good job but surely he could see what a complete mess it had turned out to be. What on earth next? If his eyes deteriorated further would I walk in on him using hedge clippers or garden shears? It was probably him that had started the trend of shaved patches in ones eyebrows.

I would often need to retire to my room to snigger, so that I didn't ruin his false impression that he had done a good job and saved money yet again. I had been in my room one time when a lot of soapy lather had begun to creep under the door gathering more and more momentum. Wash day had always been an interesting day, to say the least, in this home. Clothes could often be seen pegged on the line, with all of them the same colour, because he had never mastered the simple act of separating coloureds from whites.

On this day though, even he had taken things to a whole new level. As I came out of my room to do a little investigating, I discovered bubbles up to the ceiling and could see no further than the end of my nose. It turned out that due to us having no washing powder he had settled on plan B. He had put washing up liquid into the washing machine, because he had never used this method before, he miscalculated how much would actually be needed. He filled both drawers where the powder would normally be inserted and then just to be on the safe side he had also squirted a load onto the clothes in the machine. Are you getting the picture? All the young children on the landing had run to play outside of our front door that many bubbles were escaping through the letterbox. There would be enough to last them all through the school holidays I thought.

Oh yes, wash day would never pass without some incident! Most of the clothes he ever washed would fit ME eventually; he had shrunk them so much. I thought we would need to live upstairs for the next few days, as the never ending cycle on the machine would send out yet another allocation of suds. He never understood what a quick wash was and what a two hour routine was, buttons were buttons to him! He would press one and if it worked then he was satisfied. He never read a guide book, I doubted, his whole life. The bubbles would be fun for a while until the novelty wore off and even the small children had become bored and left. Nothing ever alarmed me no more and I'd long since appreciated I would have to deal with a minimum of two incidents a day of a serious nature and you just learn to take it in your stride.

Once or twice I had even considered taking some of his medication myself to attempt to keep my own stress levels down, because whichever incident I deemed to be extreme, it just all seemed to be all so matter of fact to him and he could never understand what all the fuss was about. We had just almost been smothered by an avalanche of bubbles you crazy bastard! That's what all the fuss was about.

I would look forward to my walks with him but also be a little more confident that there was less likelihood of being in any danger out in the wide open space. I was in my element out here and had long since been declared the undefeated champion of the estate. I feared no dog, in actual fact the bigger the dog the better. I would fight all comers and if he had ever made the mistake of letting me run free, without the leash, he would need to apologise over and over as I would race towards any dog and leap to make contact with their face ! Don't ask me why I did it! I suppose I was just very territorial in my actions, most little terriers are the same. But I'm the crème de la crème of the small terrier domain.

I'm a Jack Russell and fearless with it, the moment the front door is opened I will attack anyone within fifty yards of my home without hesitation. One time only I can remember getting a clip around my ear for overstepping the mark. We all have them in all our towns now walking about. The sort of Peruvian people I'd recognise by their brightly coloured dresses on the old females. They were always to be found walking in single file down the canal and as I bounded towards them I could hear Dad shouting "it's ok, don't panic, she only barks! And that's exactly what I'd done on many previous encounters, but on this particular day, I had actually made contact with my teeth, at the hem of her dress and as the old lady went to pull it away, screaming all the while, it it tore from her ankle to her thigh. I got a very firm clip at the back of my ear and cowered a little and Dad didn't know where to look as he swept me up and apologised. I was carried back to the flat and thrown in my room for the day, with the door closed! I had never been grounded before.

I had watched it happen to his younger grandchildren but this was going to be my first taste of solitary confinement. I put my sombrero over my head and hid my face in shame and just read a book for the rest of the day. God knows what made me do it, but I know, I must never do it again, lesson learned! Apparently, I could have been put down for that; whatever that meant! Still had pieces of the fabric in my teeth when I was released later and sent to clean my teeth; it would soon blow over, it always did!

Hey up "Silly Bollox" I thought, have you any idea how many times a week that I could ground you, your behaviour wasn't the best on the estate. But ok! I had got the message, rule number one don't rip old ladies dresses off! There would be nothing for supper that night it seemed, unless I ate the hundreds of bubbles that were still floating around within my room.

I was definitely in the bad book, I thought, as I gently gave my cuffed ear a little stroke. That had never happened before and I certainly didn't want it to happen again. The mood had lightened in the morning and everything seemed to be back to normal so I intended to ease myself back into his good books. I had tidied my room throughout the night and had used the dustpan and brush rather than running the hoover around and then I didn't disturb his sleep.

I was a good little dog really and it was very rare I misbehaved and so I think I had been given a conditional discharge for the time being. I was still allowed to fight, it seemed, because he never made no effort to break up any fracas, obviously he had begun to recognise that it was part of my nature and could not be prevented. I had promised myself I would try and help a little more around the house, starting by studying the instruction manual for the washing machine and making that duty my own.

He had been single for quite a while and he could do many practical things without difficulty. He could cook almost every meal under the sun, as people on the estate would testify, but this was only at the times when his hand functioned properly, because he had severe complications since a tendon operation. Didn't stop you clipping my ear though, you bastard, your hand worked then!

But to all intents and purposes we had a very comfortable lifestyle; I had even gone as far to comment and declare that we were in fact in an OPEN RELATIONSHIP. I have 700 friends on my page STELLA GINNELLY and all of them were pleased for me that I was being looked after and had found love at last. I was certain this adventure had many more twists and turns yet, but I'd seen just about everything I possibly could and was very much unshockable. Team Ginnelly was here to stay.

CHAPTER 27

So my friends as the story comes to a close I would hope that if I have changed even one opinion of my breed, Jack Russell's, then I would be satisfied. I have timed the completion of this book to coincide with the children being on holiday from school. I can now relax and put my paws up for a while and wait and see if it gets a favourable outcome. While I await your response to it, I will do what I always do during school breaks and spend it playing with the children and enjoying the laughter. I will obviously leave it to your own imagination what is actually fact and what is fiction. I <u>can</u> actually hold a pen and write though and that's the only clue I will give you. All of the rest is for you to decide!!

I have definitely, one million percent, visited every one of the locations mentioned within these pages and I am very lucky, to have a Dad that prefers taking me places rather than leaving me home alone or with people whose company I do not enjoy. He said we were a team and he meant every word and he has never broken even one promise he made to me. We both watched Battersea Dogs home on the TV the other night with Paul O'Grady and seen a dog that malnourished its ribs were sticking out. I jumped up on the settee and rested my head on my Dad's leg, adoringly, and looked him in the face knowing full well that I would never be mistreated to that extent.

It would always baffle me why any of you humans choose to neglect a dog to that extent, when the cost of feeding is minimal. Fortunately the dog survived, but many don't. Please, please do not even consider having a dog, unless you have the time and patience, which goes hand in hand with having one.

I have finally found my soul mate and I am given the best of everything. Clothes, food, holidays, bedding and last but not least all the love I could possibly ever ask for. I need for nothing. If any of you go on UK holidays, then give consideration to the fact your dog may also wish to go and actually deserve a break. With my obsession with water, it's all well and good having a swim in a canal or a small brook BUT nothing beats the feeling of swimming in a big sea at one of our coastlines.

Speaking of holidays one is about to take place and Bud (who remembers him) is likely to be at a loose end and in need of somewhere to stay for a week. If he thinks he is bouncing in and out of my room he is sadly mistaken. Get over it Bud, we have been over for a long time! Get yourself on Badoo or Plenty of Fish and I'm sure you will find yourself a partner just as frisky as yourself; but it won't be happening around me! I'm an old lady now and of a very similar age to Dad really, both of us wish to retire gracefully and live out our days in peace.

Neither of us sees our children, which is sad in a way but we learn to live without bitterness, such is life. Good luck to all of them and we both probably hope they have every success. Who knows maybe it's a bonus in itself not to have all of the complications that come with them. Poison is poison no matter which way it is administrated and certain people's opinions towards Dad seem toxic. I'd rather he did not listen to insults, from what are basically, his ribs and the spit out of his mouth. He is worthy of more than that. Everyone I have met in and around him admires him greatly and certainly not in a false manner. He is capable of flooding the odd kitchen and the people who live below but other than that he offends nobody and is well loved by all. Especially me!! I hope you all enjoy the book, and I will make a point of putting many of my photographs in, so that you can not only read how happy I am, but you will also be able to view what a happy little dog I am.

I could have mentioned much more, but it really is time to go because I can hear the sound of constant drilling from the living room and I can see he is drilling hole after hole in the walls. I'd like to tell you he is putting up some shelfs or doing something positive BUT I'd be lying. He is simply drilling holes for no reason, unless he is going to use the holes as a wall safe to insert all of his pills, powders and potions he needs to take each day. Ooops! He is beginning to take all his clothes off, I really need to go! From here on in I will be needed to ensure he remains indoors!! Enjoy the book. Adios Amigoes!! All my love Stella! Remember to always show kindness and especially to dogs, having wealth means little or nothing in our world.

Our favourite word is austerity because Dad and I are very much desert trained and no amount of measures that you impose on us will break our spirit. We have very little but what we do have we share with others and them are the qualities that having untold wealth will never bring you. My only concern is the big pan of boiling oil Dad keeps on a constant low heat on the cooker, because he assures everyone who wants to listen that it will be tipped over the landing and onto anyone who tries to take our home from us. Having known him as long as I have, I can indeed confirm he is capable of acts such as this. I would be there at his side and in actual fact I have begun to sharpen my teeth with a nail file. Let the battle commence! I wish it could be Boris Johnson who would show up to try and evict us because he could definitely do with a little chip oil in his hair. We laugh and laugh at him anytime he comes on the TV because of his silly mannerisms and his hair blowing in all directions. He could learn a lot from big Donald Trump whose hair never moves a centimetre; it's got that much lacquer on it. It would be even more comical, but for the fact these are the most recent ones, who are in positions of power and responsible for our well-being. There is honestly no hope for none of us I'm afraid, L.O.L.

Dad and I never ever have any money but we are richer than anyone thinks, you learn much more about yourself living life at the bottom. We had long since accepted this is the way it was to be and the situation could not be changed so you very quickly accept your lot and make the most of it. When the life around you involves much lunacy, then it soon becomes easy to disregard what is reality. No set game plan so to speak. Wake up and spend the day being mentally unbalanced and your cares and worries will soon go out of the window. It only becomes a problem if the furniture goes out of the window!! L.O.L. I have witnessed the bedside cabinets go hurtling past the bay window from the upstairs bedroom, and with previous incidents with the TV and other items. I would laugh and think the resident living below, could open up a second hand shop, with all of the furniture Dad had thrown from the flat.

I can hear him now upstairs and still with the drill in his hand, making yet more holes in the bathroom, so I will need to check on him shortly and take his medication up to him. If he really wanted to do something positive with that bleeding drill, I would readily suggest a lobotomy, would perhaps be beneficial. I will need to finish off now but you have surely realised that the adventures of Tin Tin, haven't got a patch on my life. Here's hoping too many more years of madness and mayhem. I wouldn't swap it for the world, it's the reason my tail wags each day!!

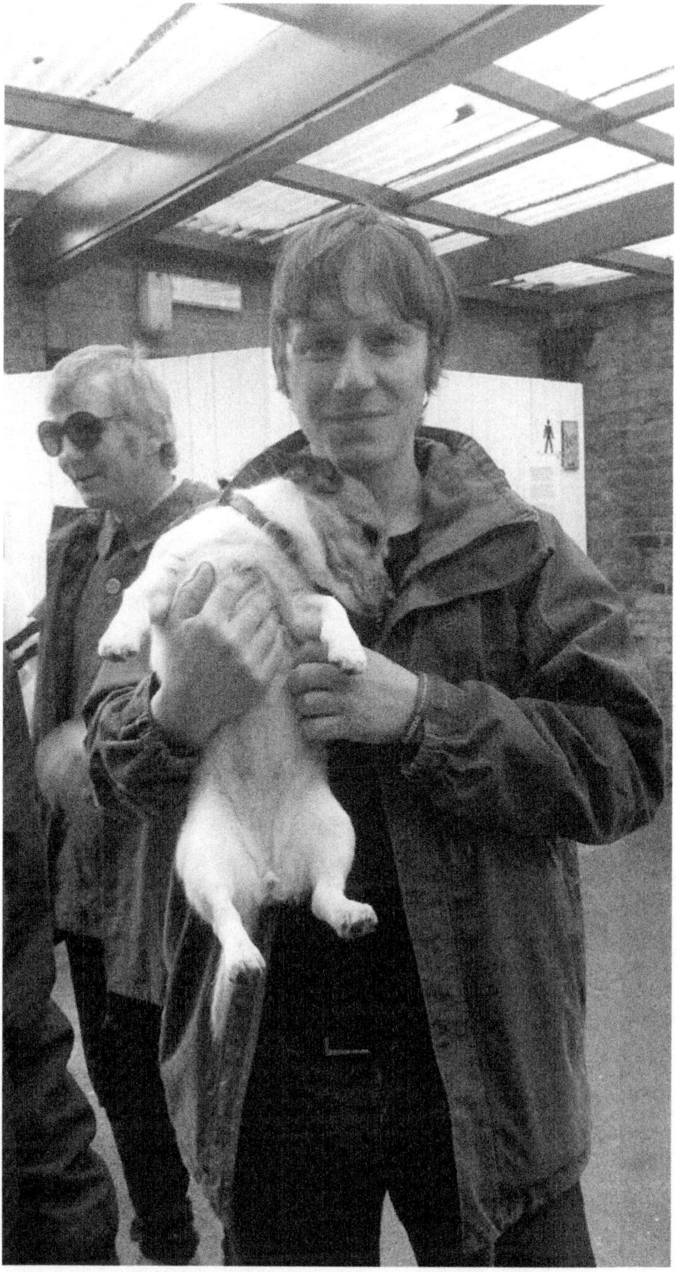

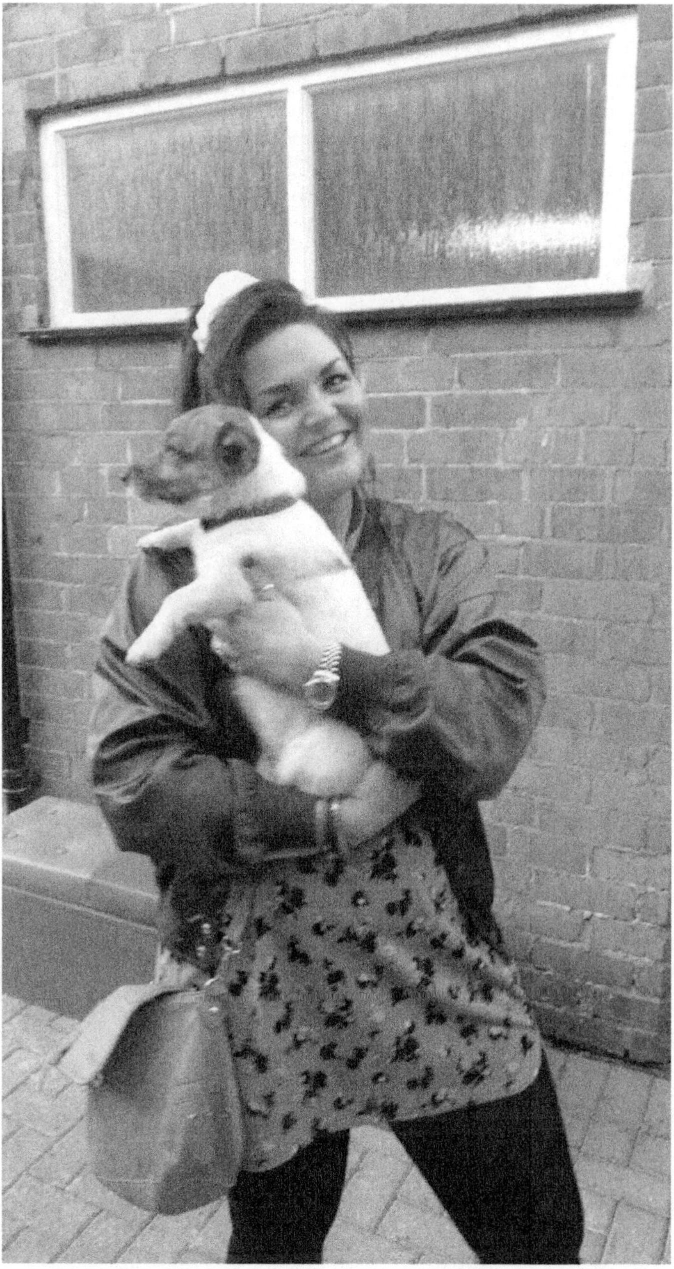

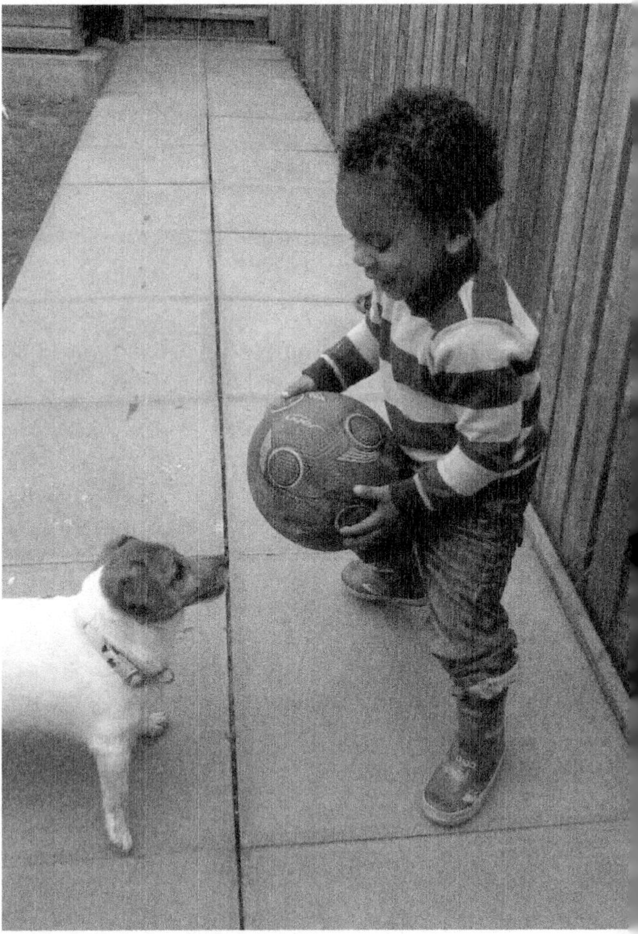

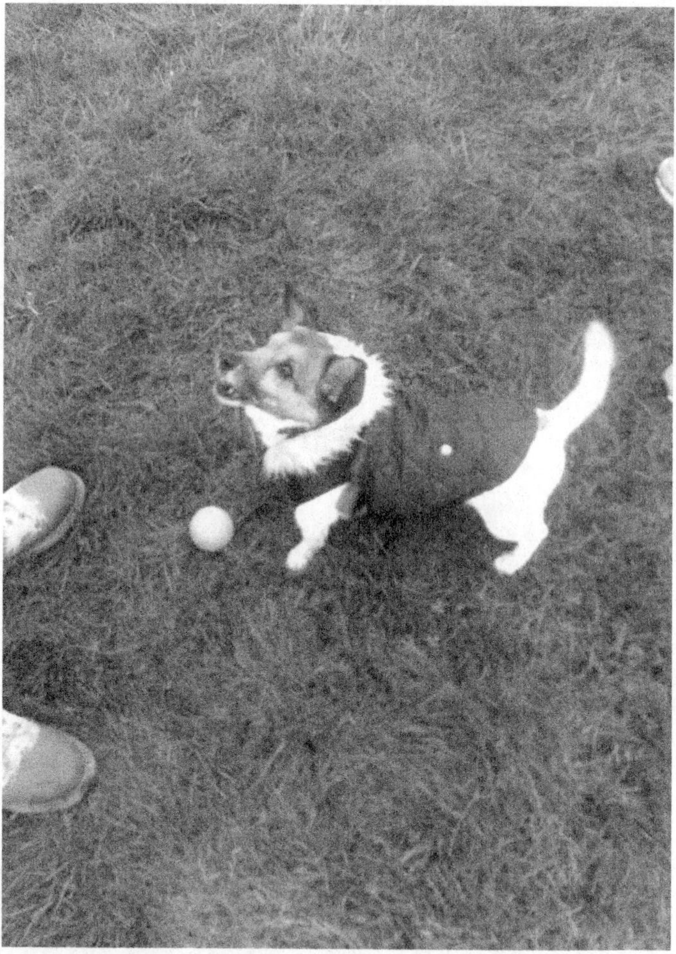

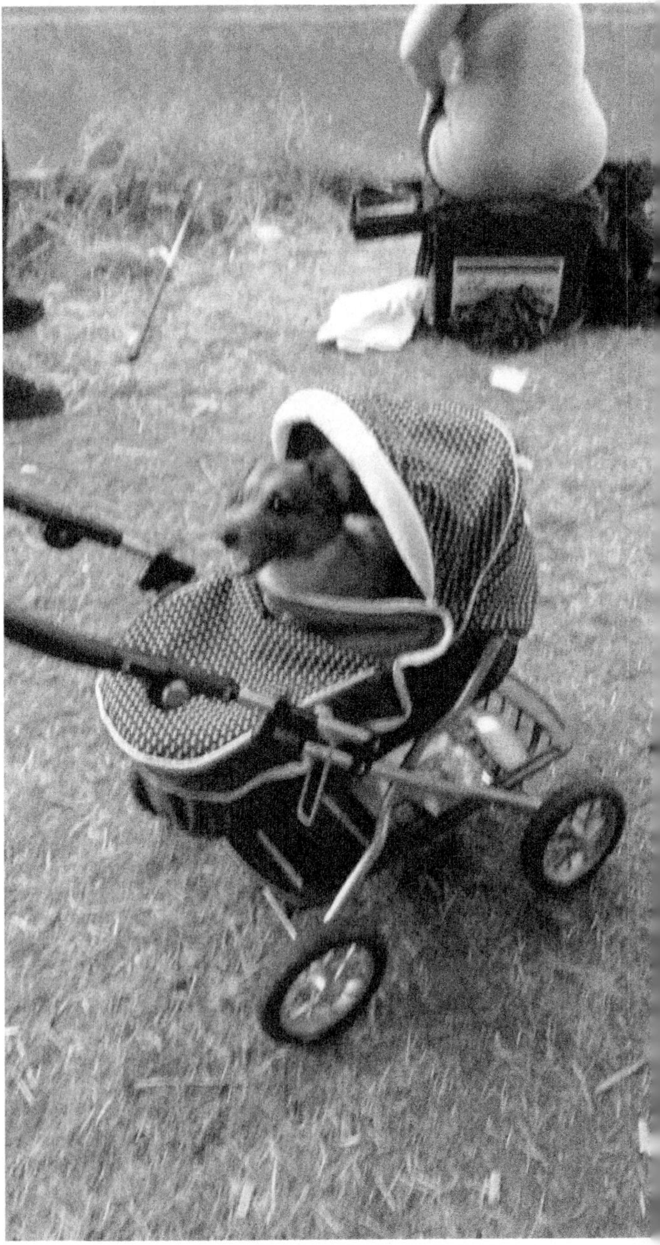

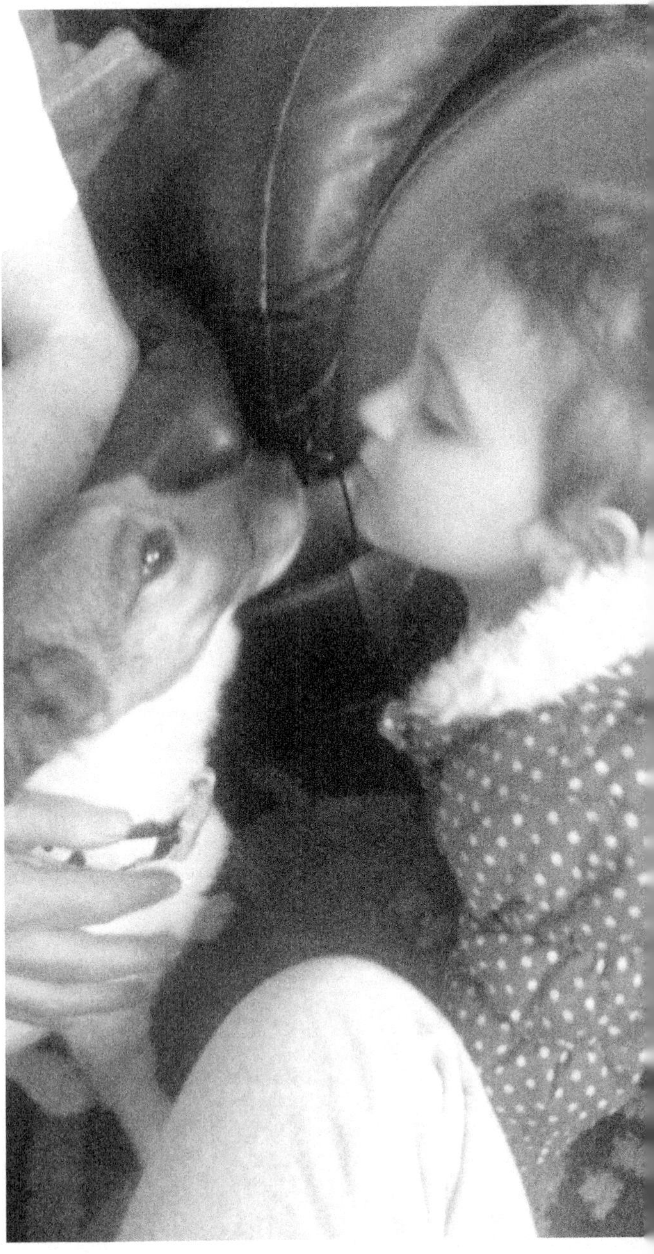

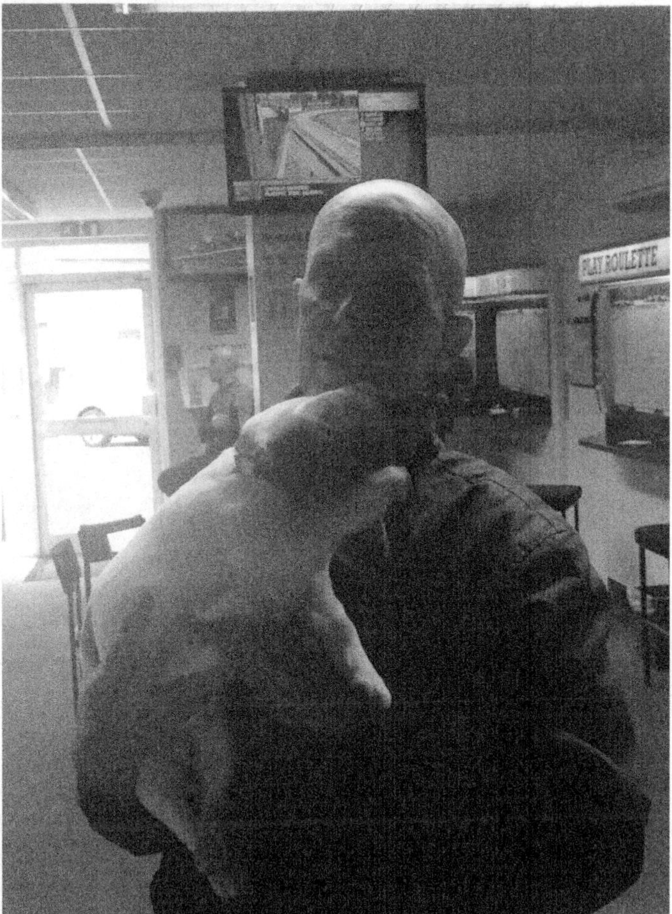
PLAY ROULETTE

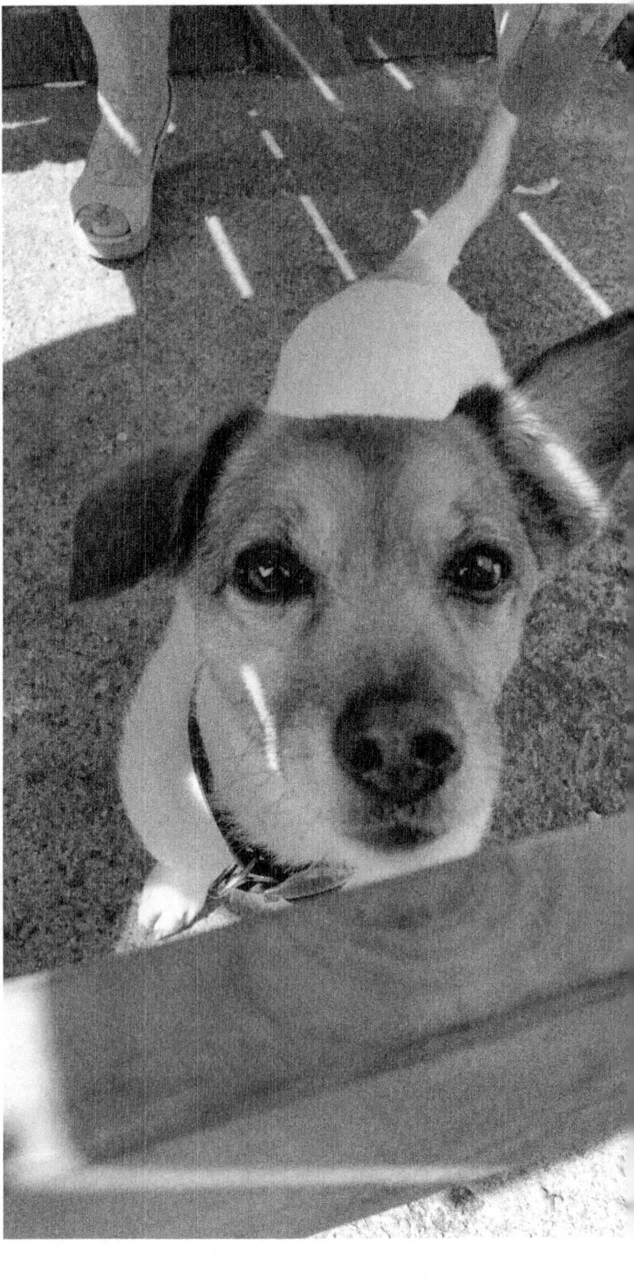

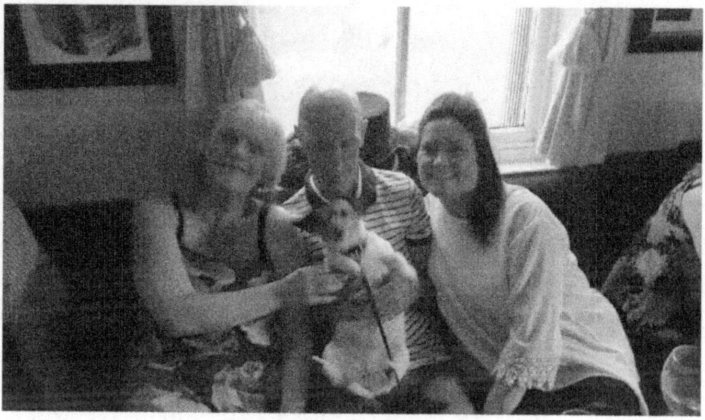

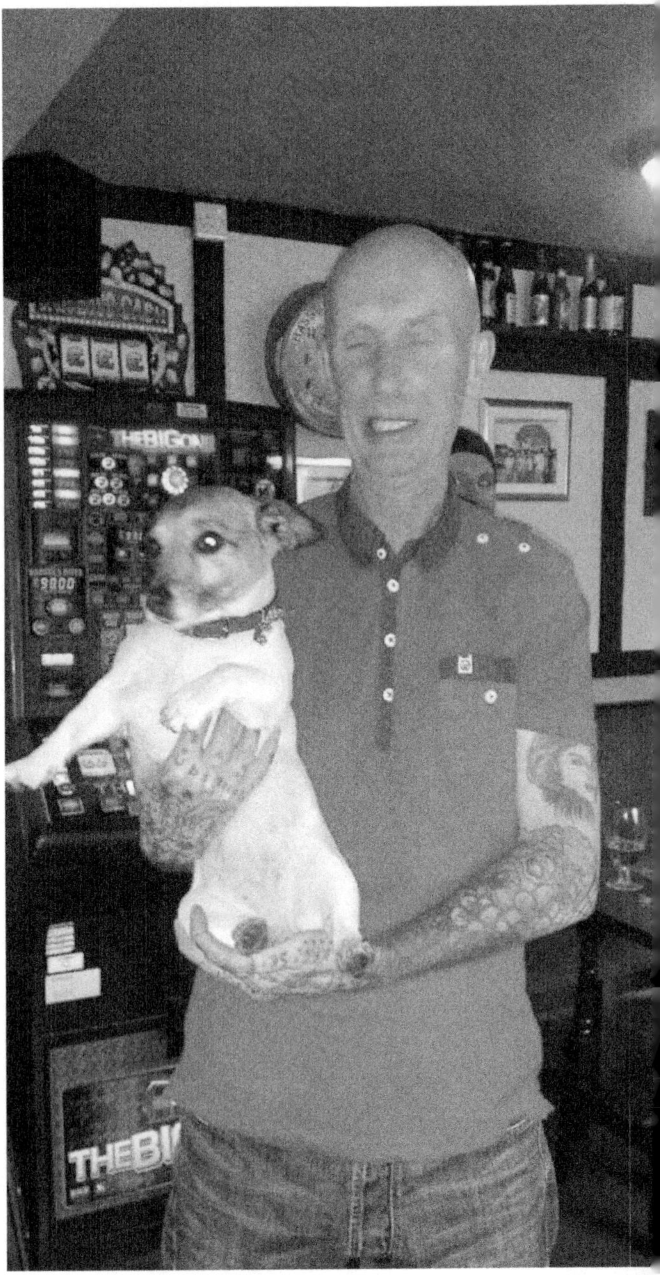
THEBIGON
THEBI

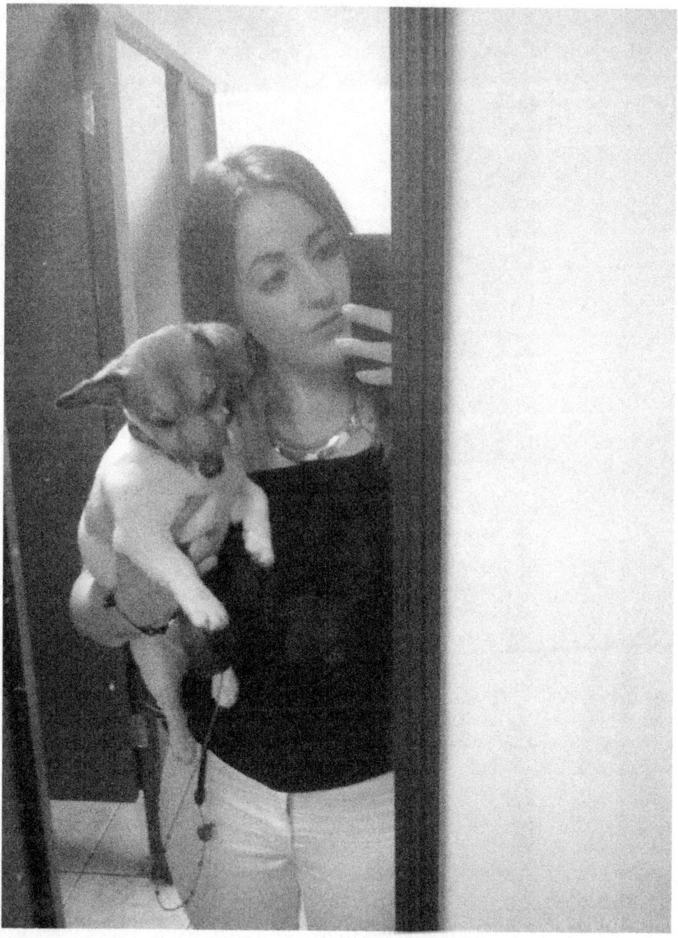

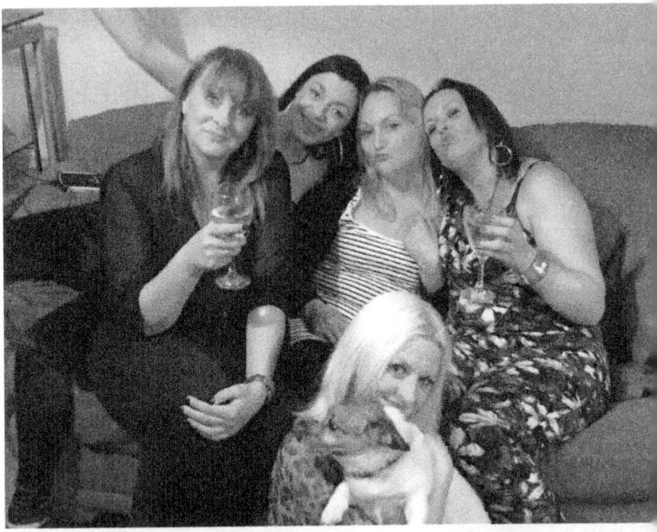

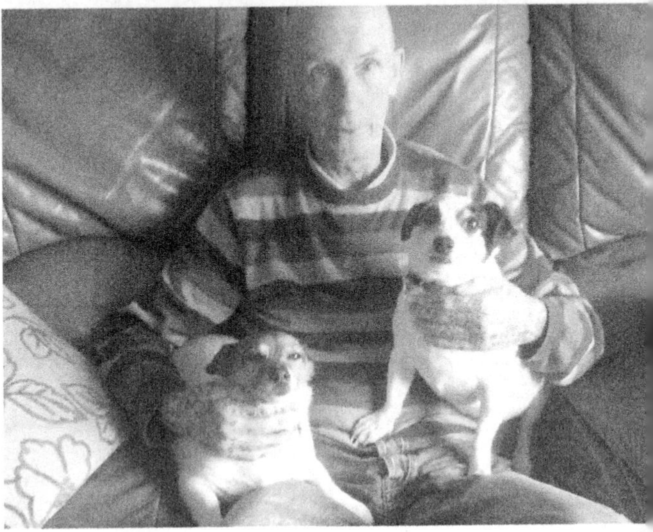

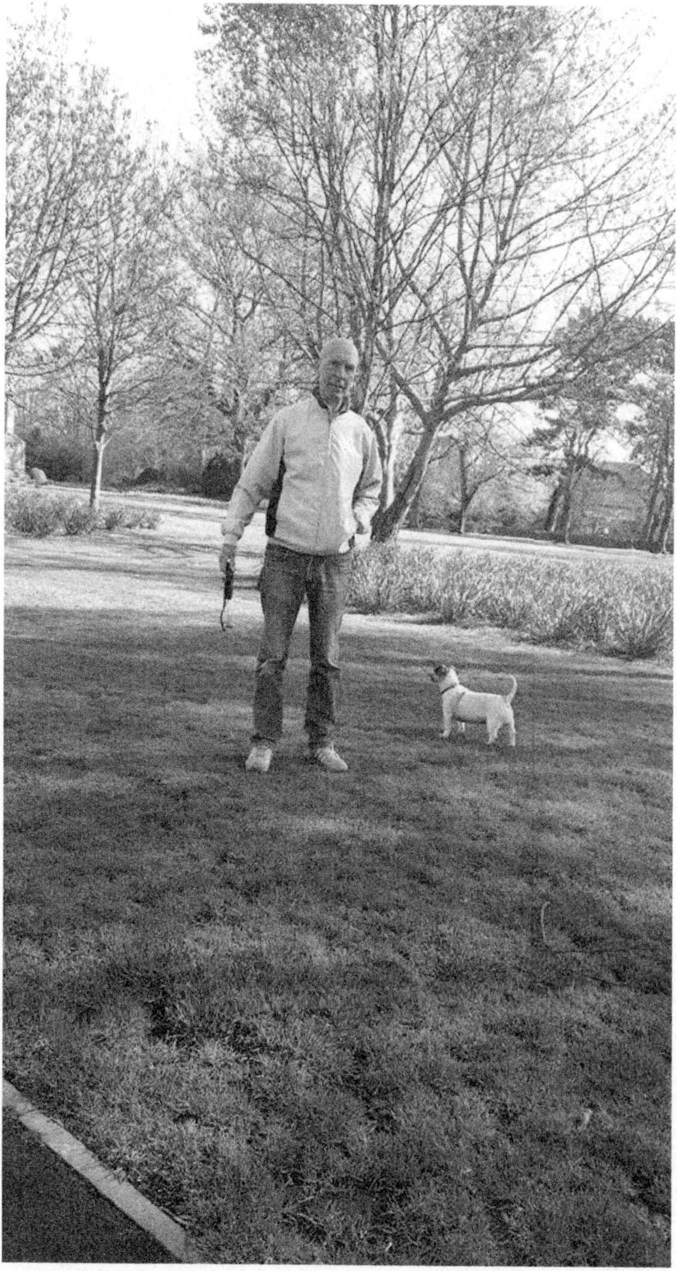

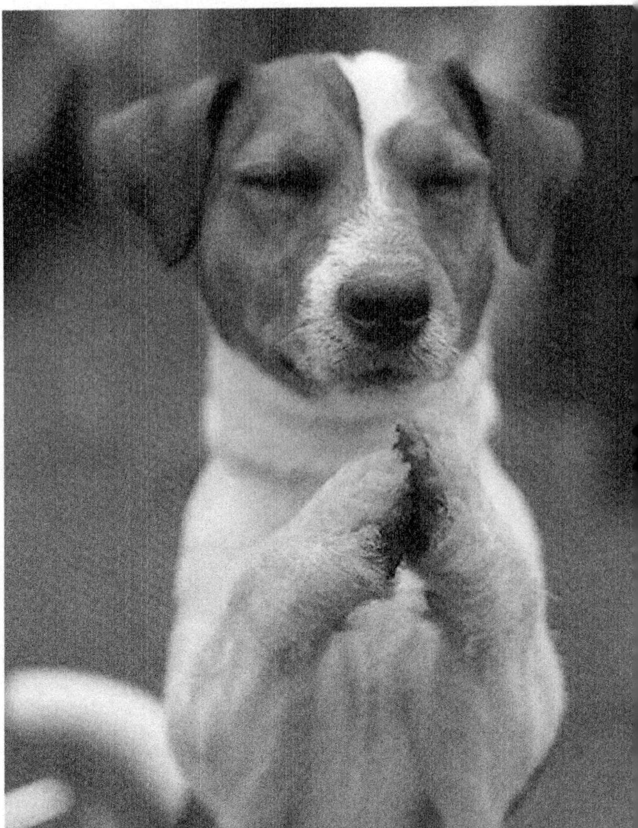

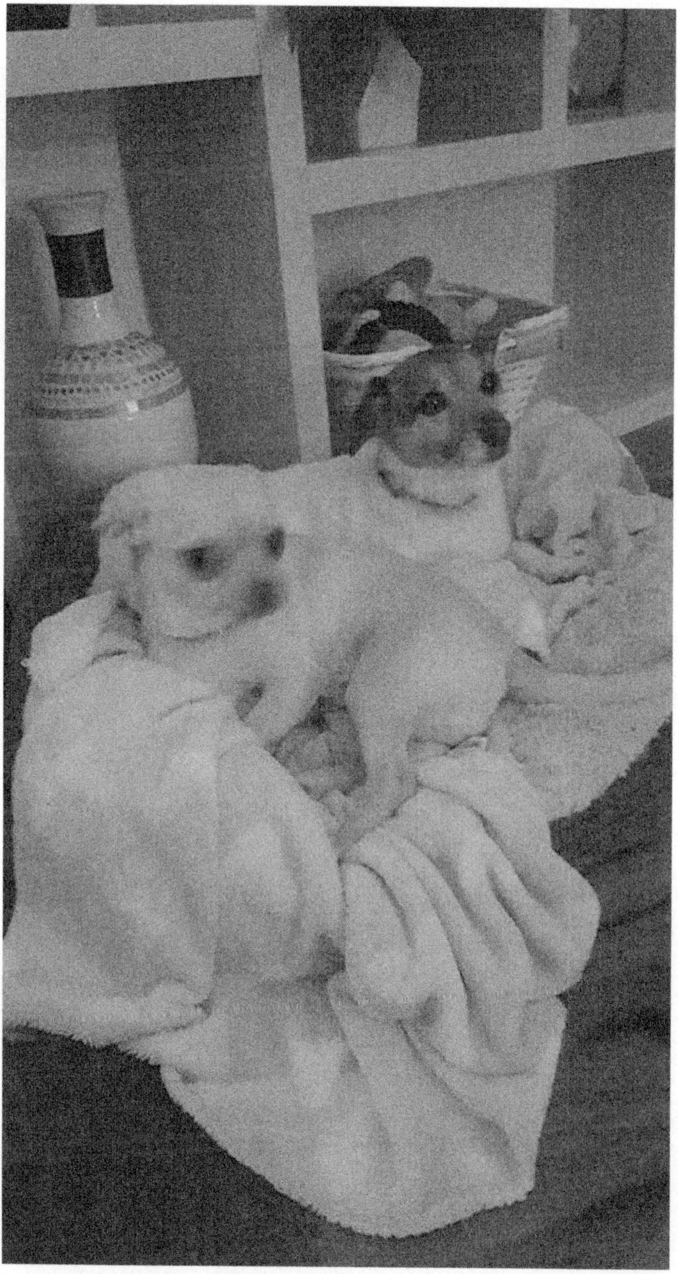

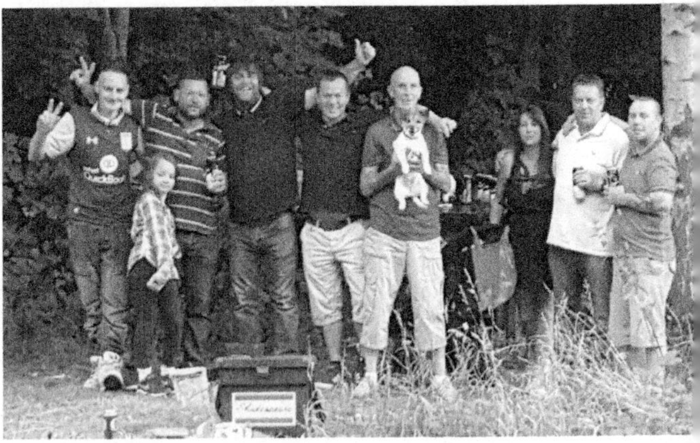

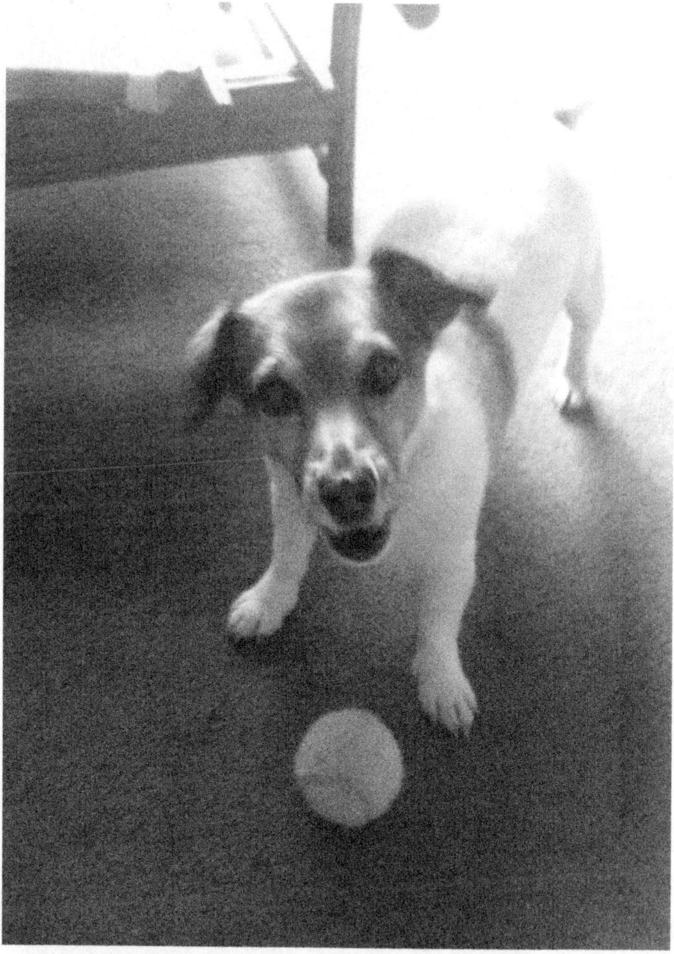

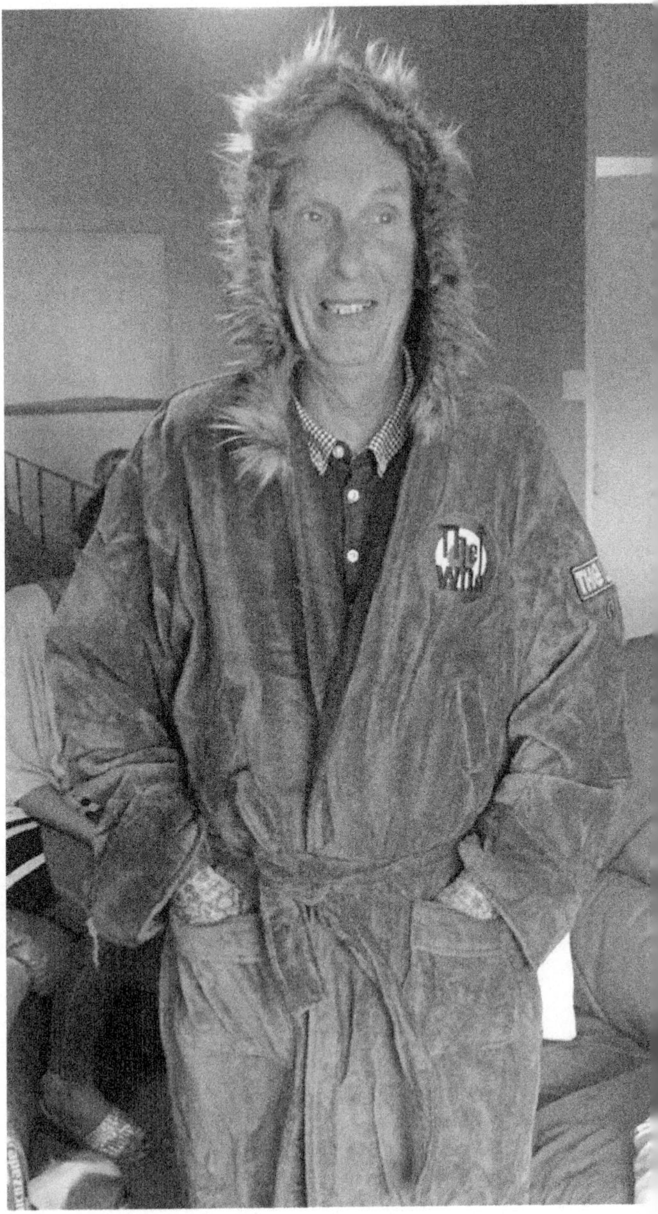

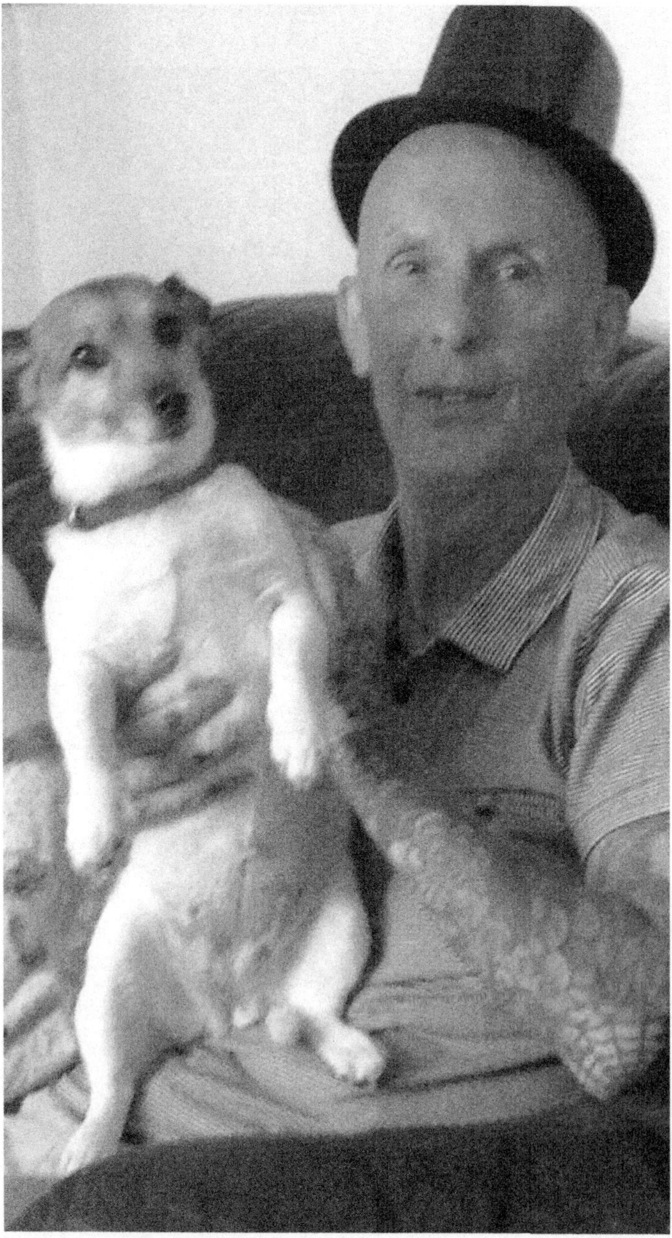

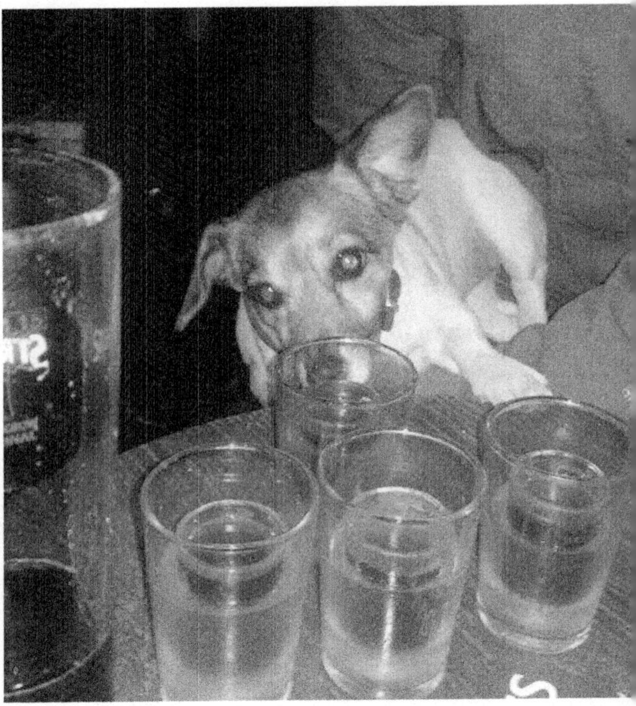

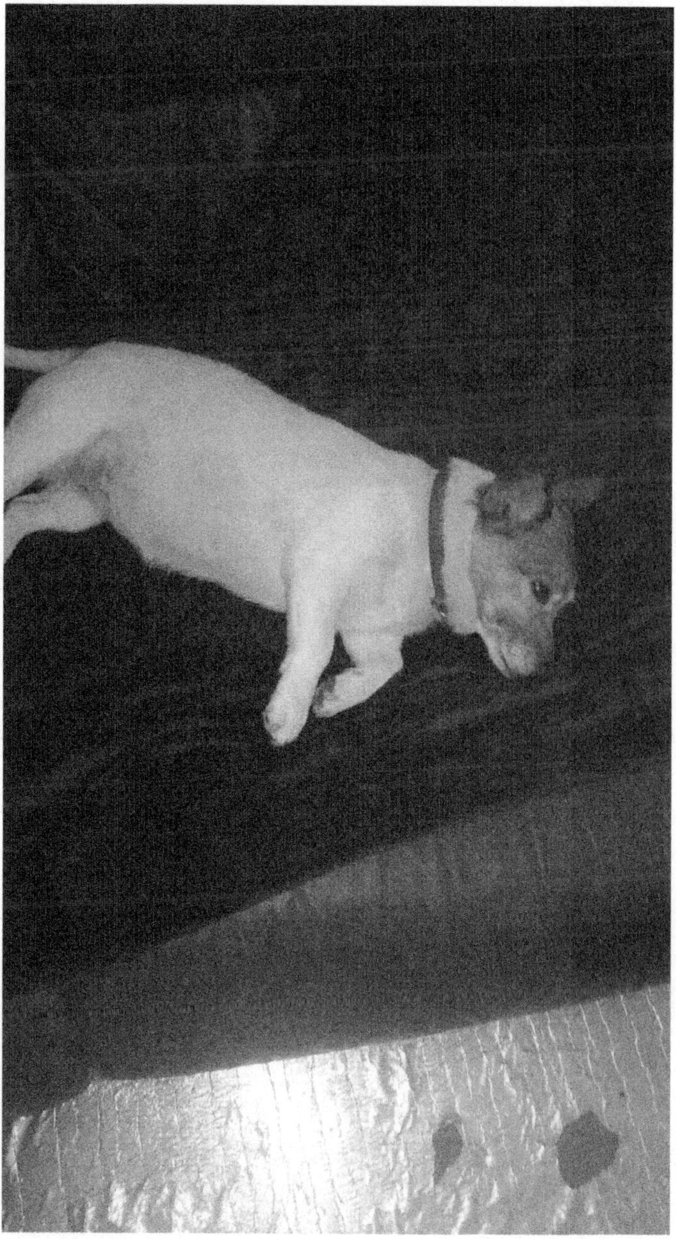

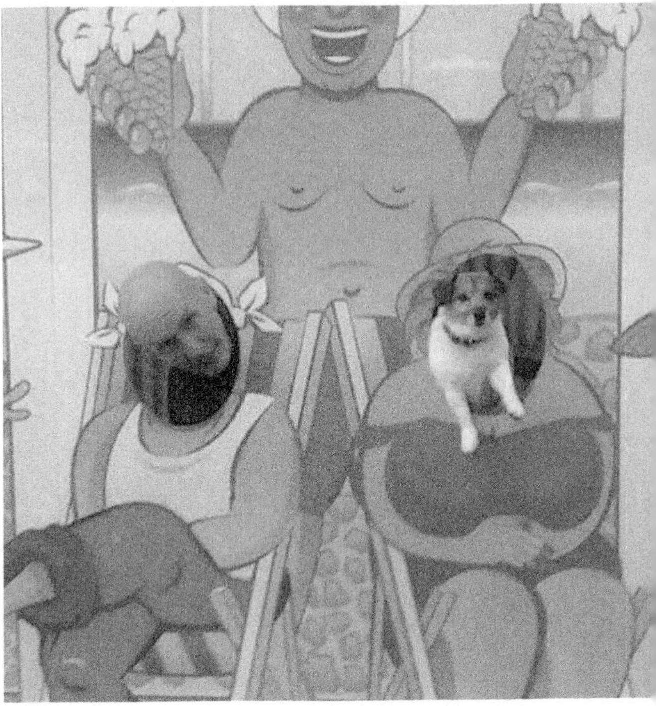

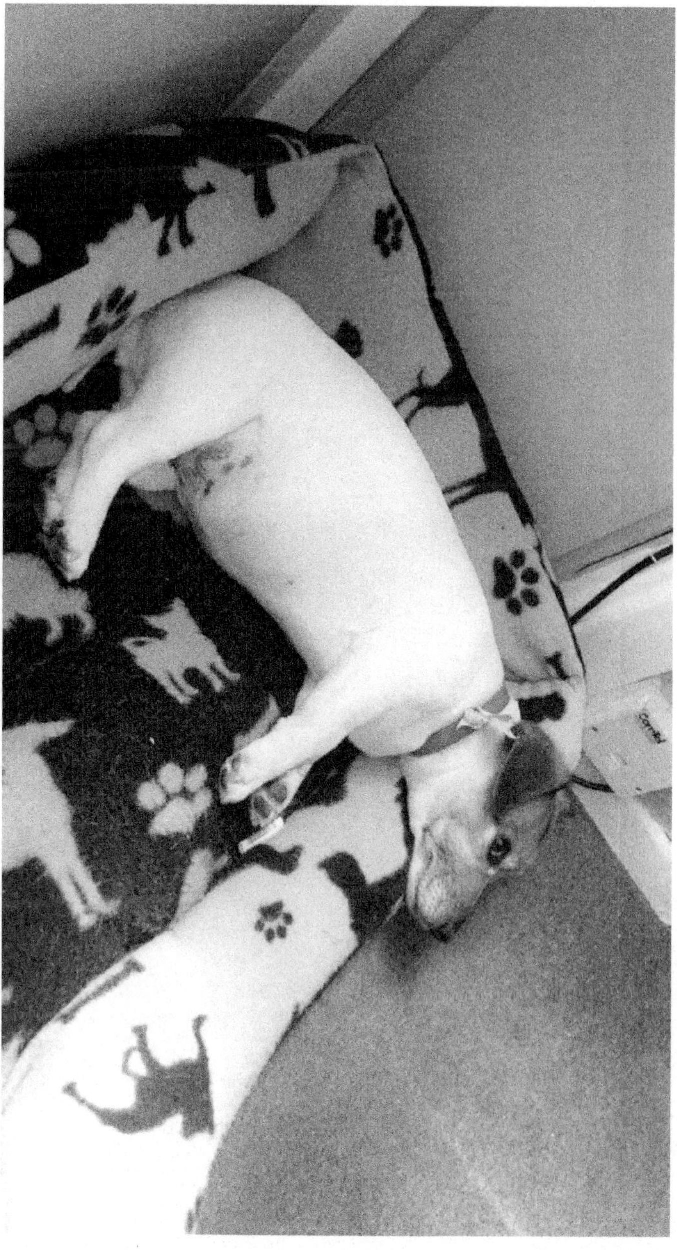

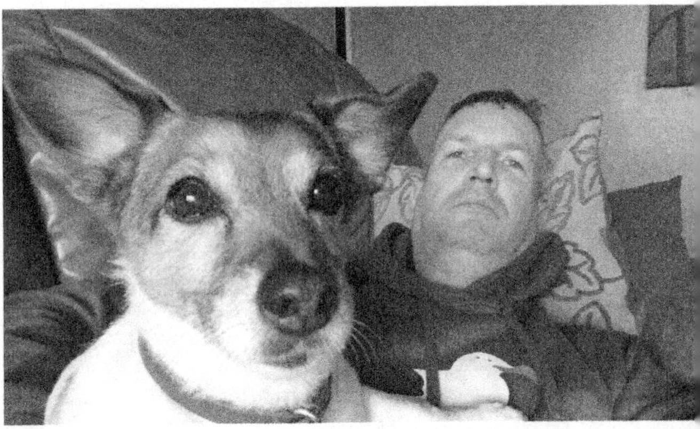

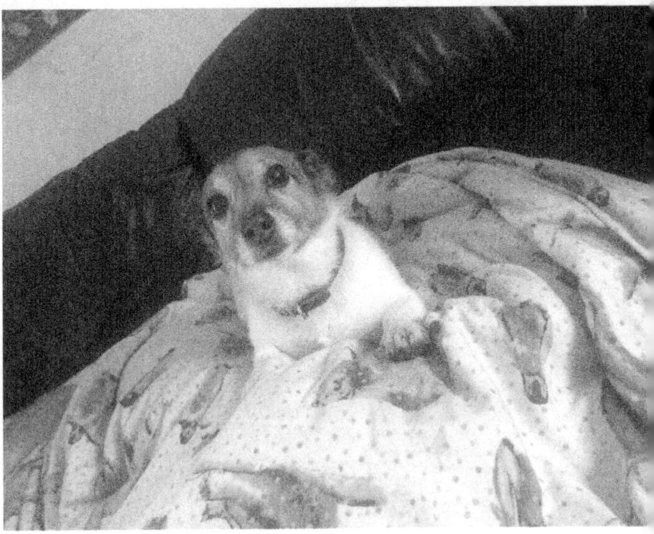

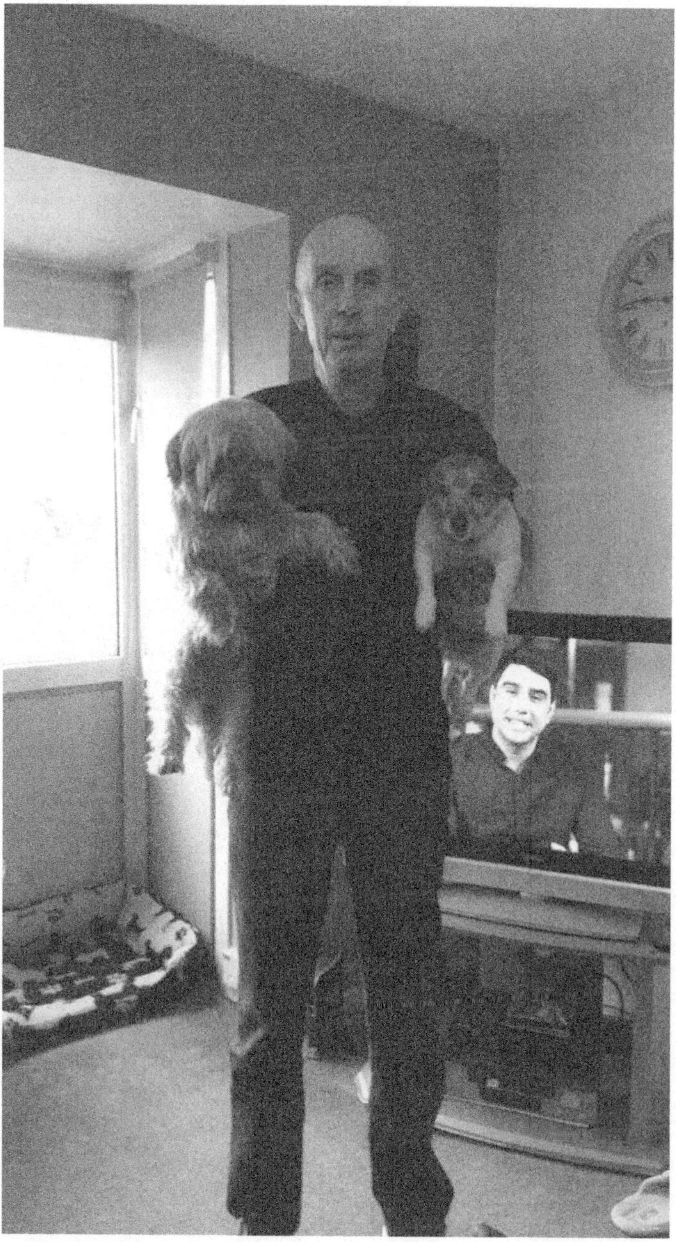

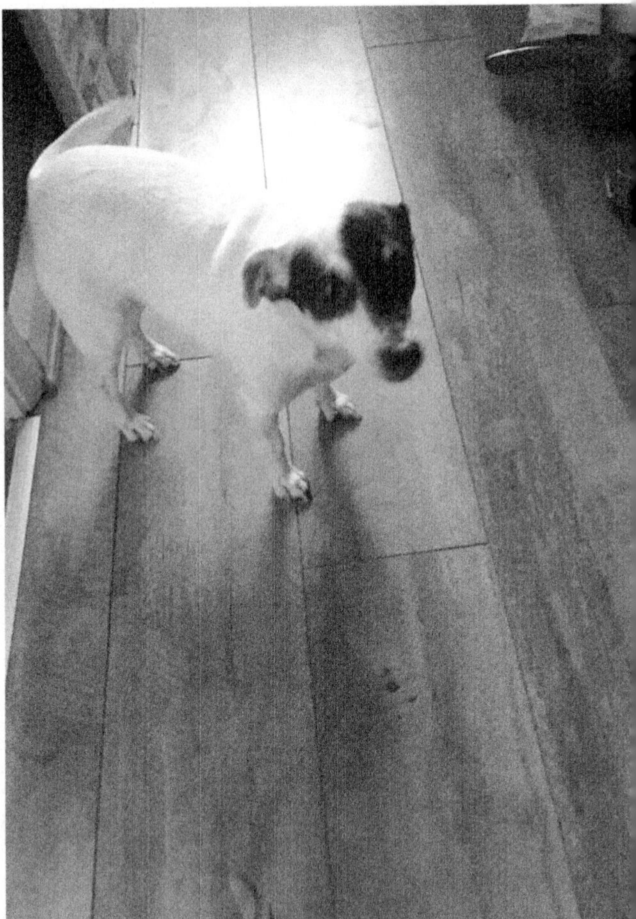

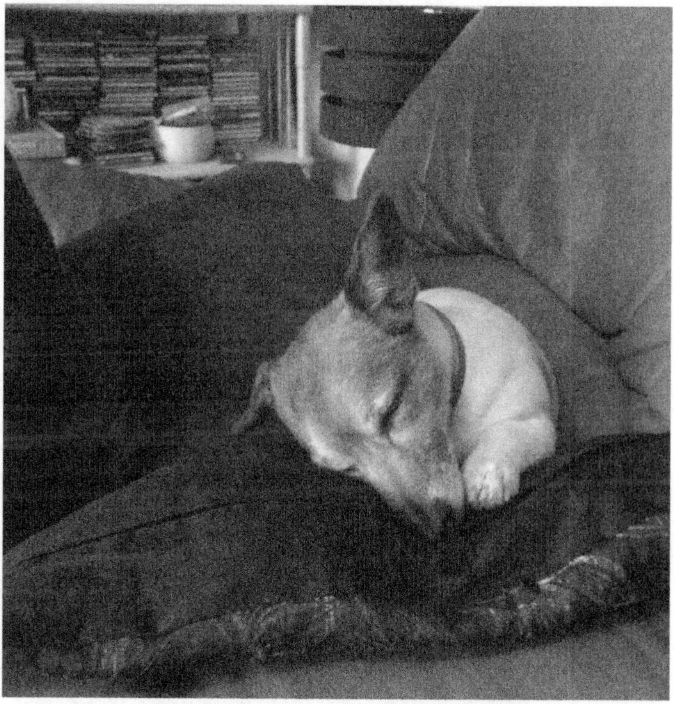

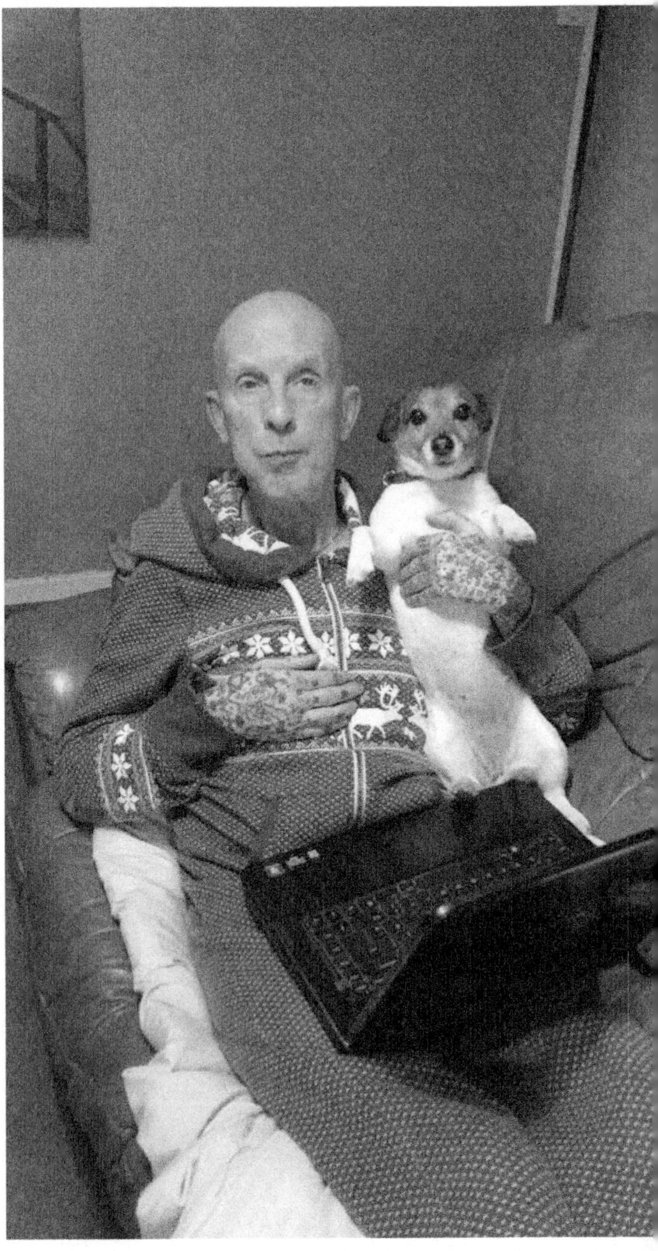

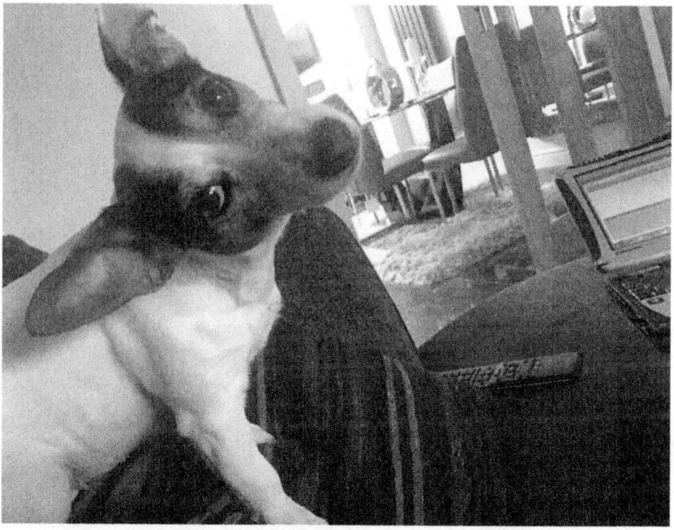

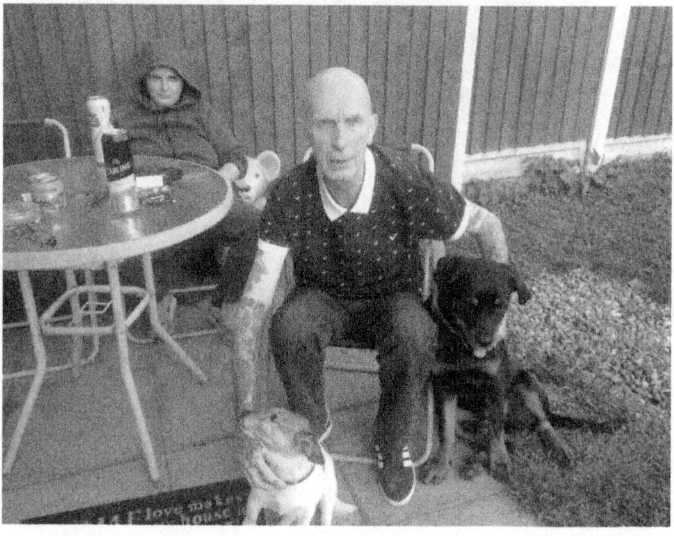

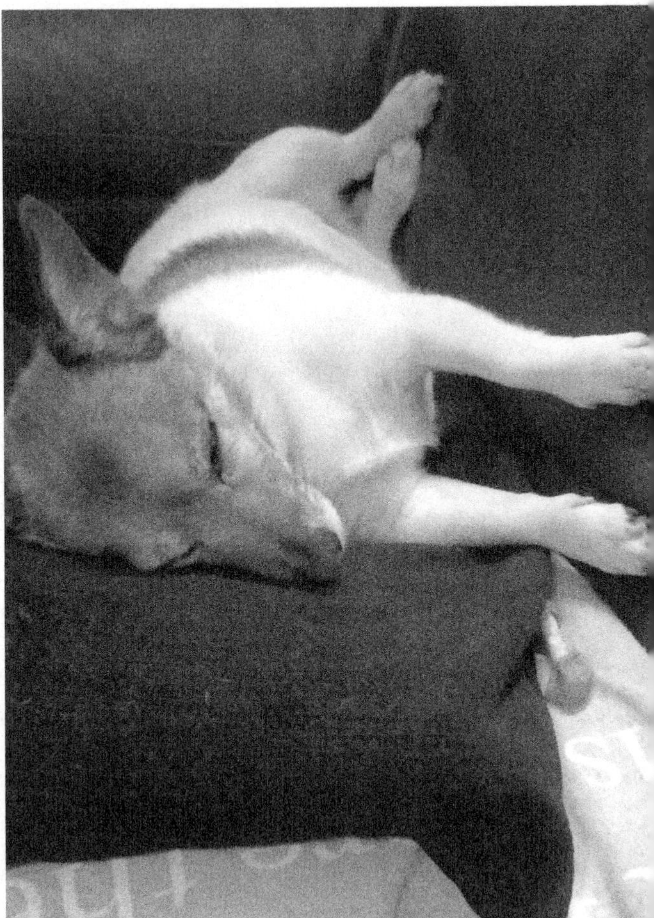

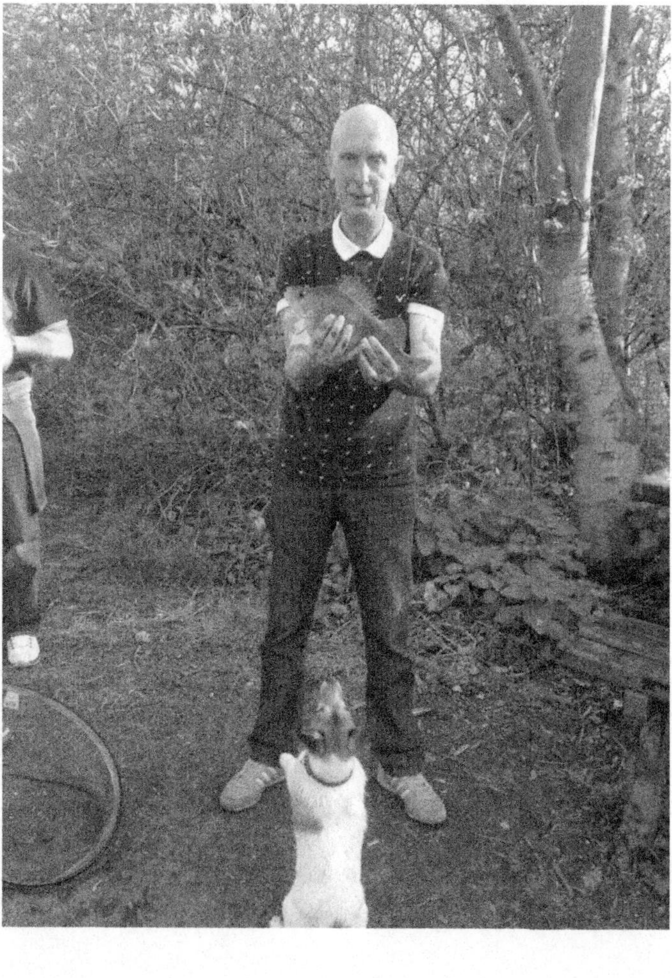

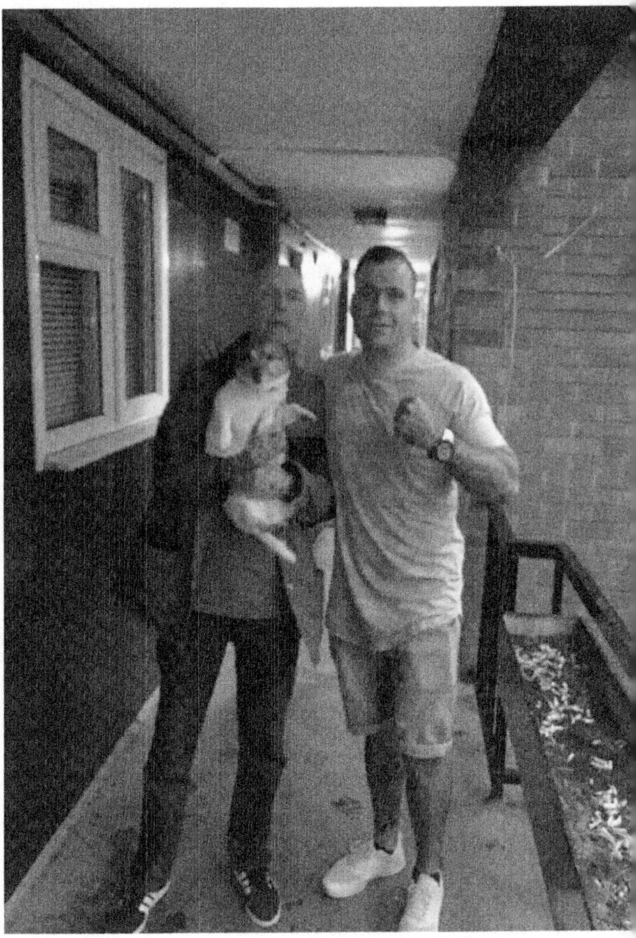

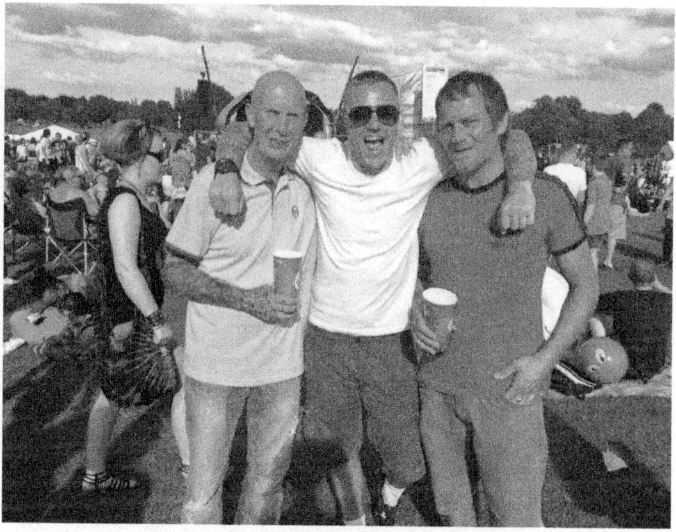

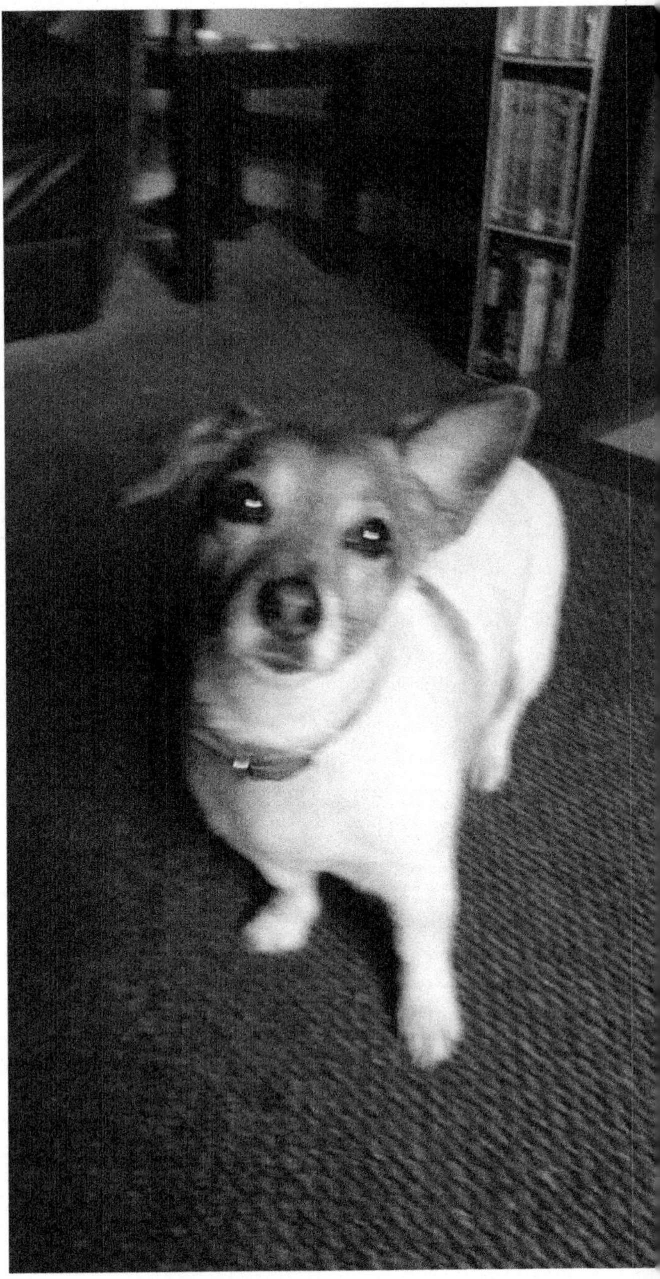

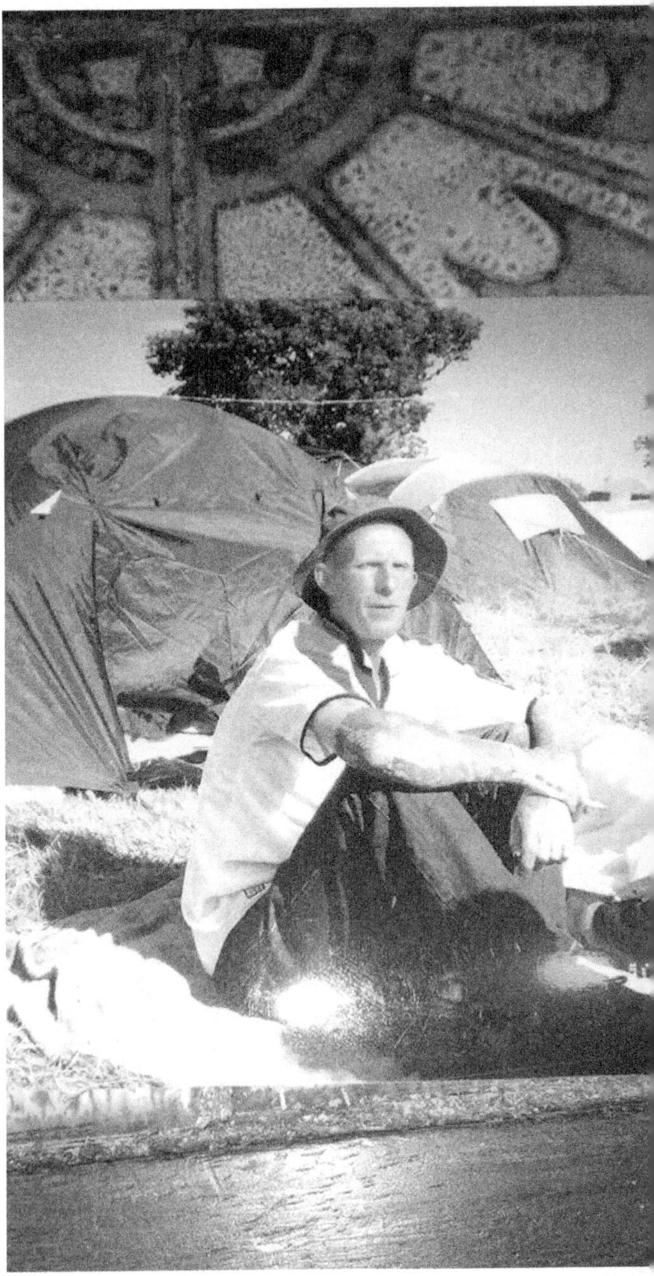